Rastafari: Beliefs & Principles

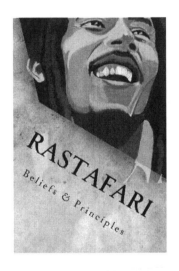

by

Empress Yuajah

ISBN-10: 149484656X
ISBN-13: 978-1494846565

Life as a Rasta Woman

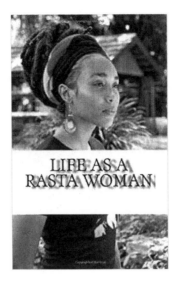

Jah Prayers   **Rastafari**

Rasta Way of Life

How to Become a Rasta

Convert to Rastafari

Ital Rasta eCookbook

King Selassie I Speech:

New Way of Life

A new way of life. We search for a way of life in which all men will be treated as responsible human beings, able to participate fully in the political affairs of their government; a way of life in which ignorance and poverty, if not abolished, are at least the exception and are actively combatted; a way of life in which the blessings and benefits of the modern world can be enjoyed by all without the total sacrifice of all that was good and beneficial in the old Ethiopia. We are from and of the people, and our desires derive from and are theirs.

Can this be achieved from one dusk to the next dawn, by the waving of a magic wand, by slogans or by Imperial declaration? Can this be imposed on our people, or be achieved solely by legislation? We believe not. All that we can do is provide a means for the development of procedures which, if all goes well, will enable an increasing measure and degree of what we seek for our nation to be accomplished. Those who will honestly and objectively view the past history of this nation cannot but be impressed by what has already been realised during their lifetime, as well as be awed by the magnitude of the problems which still remain.

Annually, on this day, we renew our vow to labour, without thought of self, for so long as Almighty God shall spare us, in the service of our people and our nation, in seeking the solutions to these problems. We call upon each of you and upon each Ethiopian to do likewise......

Above all, Ethiopia is dedicated to the principle of the equality of all men, irrespective of differences of race, colour or creed.

As we do not practice or permit discrimination within our nation, so we oppose it wherever it is found.

As we guarantee to each the right to worship as he chooses, so we denounce the policy which sets man against man on issues of religion.

As we extend the hand of universal brotherhood to all, without regard to race or colour, so we condemn any social or political order which distinguishes among God's children on this most specious of grounds.

DEDICATION

To Bob Marley

For the Great Rastafari Bob Marley, Musician and Messenger of Jah. Thank you for opening the doors for other Rastafari to teach and share Rastafari.

To Jah

Thank you Jah. You have given me the greatest gift any human could ever have. I am in awe of your love and your power every day.

Thanks and praises unto The Most High, Jah Rastafari.

Table of Contents

Rastafari is a spirituality of the heart. If you use your mind to understand something that is spiritual, you may miss the true essence and meaning of it.

As you read this book, know that facts and dates is not what Rastafari is about. Rastafari is a feeling, the feeling of Jah, Jah Love, and the relationship between him and his covenanted people.

May Jah bless you and guide you, that your heart may be opened, and your spirit may be filled with Rastafari knowledge, wisdom, and "Overstanding."

Unity & Blessed Love. Rastafari.

[2] As the sun was going down, a deep sleep fell on Abram. And behold, dreadful and great darkness fell upon him. [13] Then the Lord said to Abram, "Know for certain that your offspring will be sojourners in a land that is not theirs and will be servants there, and they will be afflicted for four hundred years. [14] But I will bring judgment on the nation that they serve, and afterward they shall come out with great possessions. [15] As for you, you shall go to your fathers in peace; you shall be buried in a good old age. [16] And they shall come back here in the fourth generation, for the iniquity of the Amorites is not yet complete."

"Overstanding"
"...My people are destroyed for lack of knowledge..." - <u>Hosea 4:6-7</u>

What's to "Overstand" about Rastafari?

If you embrace Rastafari without the **awareness that Black people have struggled and still struggle today,** then you really are not embracing the Rastafari faith as it truly is.

Rastafari is born of "the black struggle!" You can't say you did not know. Let me repeat that. Rastafari was *born of* "the black struggle," and the black nation still "struggle" today because of some very key components rarely discussed.

Rastafari is a spiritual "secret"

Rastafari is a "knowing"... Much of what I know as Rasta Empress is not written in books. Besides, Babylon wants all of us to be like robots...without our own thoughts, just following along... knowing only what they want us to know, and doing only what they want us to do.

Rastafari wisdom and "Overstanding," comes from Jah, and has been secretly written on the Rastafari heart at his/her conception! Yes at his/her conception!!! It is our Job as Rastafari (prophets) to share that truth and bring the light to the people....to help them to "Overstand" Jah light, and Jah living – Rastafari!

Beginning of "the black struggle"

The truth is the beginning of the "black struggle" started during biblical times in Egypt when the people of Israel were "servants" to the Egyptians as promised to Abraham(Abram) by Jah.

A life of Slavery (Servitude)
Genesis 15

[12] As the sun was going down, a deep sleep fell on Abram. And behold, dreadful and great darkness fell upon him. [13] Then the Lord said to Abram, "Know for certain that your offspring will be sojourners in a land that is not theirs and will be servants there, and they will be afflicted for four hundred years. [14] But I will bring judgment on the nation that they serve, and afterward they shall come out with great possessions. [15] As for you, you shall go to your fathers in peace; you shall be buried in a good old age. [16] And they shall come back here in the fourth generation, for the

iniquity of the Amorites is not yet complete."

The Israelites Oppressed - *Exodus 1*

"...1 these are the names of the (12) sons of Israel who went to Egypt with Jacob, each with his family: *2 Reuben, Simeon, Levi and Judah; 3 Issachar, Zebulun and Benjamin; 4 Dan and Naphtali, Gad, and Asher. 5 The descendants of Jacob numbered seventy[a] in all; Joseph was already in Egypt.

6 Now Joseph and all his brothers and all that generation died, 7 but the Israelites were exceedingly fruitful; they multiplied greatly, increased in numbers and became so numerous that the land was filled with them.

8 Then a new king, to whom Joseph meant nothing, came to power in Egypt. 9 "Look," he said to his people, "the Israelites have become far too numerous for us. 10 Come, we must deal shrewdly with them or

they will become even more numerous and, if war breaks out, will join our enemies, fight against us and leave the country."

<u>¹¹ So they put slave masters over them to oppress</u> them with forced labor, and they built Pithom and Rameses as store cities for Pharaoh. ¹² But the more they were oppressed, the more they multiplied and spread; so the Egyptians came to dread the Israelites ¹³ and worked them ruthlessly. ¹⁴ They made their lives bitter with harsh labor in brick and mortar and with all kinds of work in the fields; in all their harsh labor the Egyptians worked them ruthlessly..."

The Burning Bush
(Moses Initiated as Jah Prophet)`

3 Now Moses was tending the flock of Jethro his father-in-law, the priest of Midian, and he led the flock to the far side of the wilderness and came to Horeb, the mountain of God. ² There the angel of the Lord appeared to him in flames of fire from within a bush. Moses saw that though the bush was on fire it did not burn up. ³ So Moses thought, "I will go over and see this

strange sight—why the bush does not burn up."

⁴ When the Lord saw that he had gone over to look, God called to him from within the bush, "Moses! Moses!"

And Moses said, "Here I am."

⁵ "Do not come any closer," God said. "Take off your sandals, for the place where you are standing is holy ground." ⁶ Then he said, "I am the God of your father, [a] the God of Abraham, the God of Isaac and the God of Jacob." At this, Moses hid his face, because he was afraid to look at God.

The Lord said...

"I have indeed seen the misery of <u>my people</u> in Egypt. I have heard them crying out because of their slave drivers, and I am concerned about their suffering. ⁸ So I have come down to rescue them from the hand of the Egyptians and to bring them up out of that land into a good and spacious land, a land flowing with milk and honey—the home of the Canaanites, Hittites, Amorites,

Perizzites, Hivites and Jebusites. [9] And now <u>the cry of the Israelites has reached me,</u> and I have seen the way the Egyptians are oppressing them. [10] So now, go. I am sending you to Pharaoh to bring my people the Israelites out of Egypt."

And so Rastafari began...
Jah hears the cries of his people, and
He appoints a prophet - Moses, to lead them out of their slavery and oppression.

How to Dress as a Rasta Empress

Typically Rasta women do not wear shiny jewelry. We prefer to wear Rasta earrings, Rasta rings, Rasta bracelets, and necklaces that are made of wood, or shell, copper, seeds (natural) or beaded, and that have a more natural appearance.

Dreadlocks Rasta Hair

Rasta women wear their hair in dreadlocks; you cannot call yourself a Rasta and have loose hair that is just not going to work. We keep our hair in locks, and we do not curl it or put color in it, only maybe to cover up grey hairs, but that's it. We keep chemicals to a minimum too. Typically Rasta women do not "re-twist" their locks, but if you do this it is ok.

Rasta Clothing

There is a lot of nice Rasta clothing that can be found online for Rasta women. Much Rasta clothing for women comes in red yellow and green, and is usually in the form of a dress or a skirt. Deep Rasta women do not wear pants. You can wear your own clothes as long as they are clean and comfortable and not revealing. Please no skirts above the knee, and no low-cut tank tops.

Rasta Shoes

Any type of shoe is allowed as long as it is not too high of a heel or not too shiny. You be the judge.

A Rasta Woman's Makeup

Make up must be kept to a minimum and only for work or special occasions. No bright colors please. Rasta women respect Jah and we like to share our natural beauty with the world.

Hair wrap

There are many hair wraps for Rasta women which can be bought online.

5 Reasons Rastafari Women Cover Their Locks in Public

A true Rasta woman covers her hair to show spiritual respect to the Most High and other deep Rasta.

A true Rastafari woman covers her locks to maintain a private spiritual relationship with only the creator, while in public!

A true Rasta woman covers her dreadlocks while in public to reserve some of her beauty only for her Rasta King and her family and herself.

A true Rasta woman wraps her hair in an upward spiral to provide more of a Queen appearance (as they do in parts Africa)

A true Rasta woman covers her hair to keep private that part of her that is holy and sacramental.

How to Dress as a True Rasta King

Rasta men wear many different kinds of Rasta jewelry and Rasta accessories. Most of the Rasta men I've seen wearing Rasta jewelry like to keep it simple unless they are going to a Rastafari, African or Caribbean event. The more Rasta or African the event, the more colorful and larger the jewelry. Many Rastafari men like to wear a pendent of the "Lion of Judah", or Emperor Haile Selassie around their neck. Some Rasta likes to sport the Rasta flag or the Jamaican flag symbol too.

Dreadlocks Rasta Hair

A true Rasta man does not twist / retwist his dreadlocks. This is especially true of Rasta men who were born in The Caribbean. However this is not a crime if it works better for your hair type. Most of the Rasta men I have seen in my town have medium to thick sized locks and it makes them look imperial masculine and sexy. True Rasta man let their facial hair grow long too. Please if you do have facial hair and plan to let it grow long right to the ground like a true Rasta man, please keep it groomed, we women will appreciate it.

An Experience:

I once met a man who called himself Rasta, who allowed his beard to grow into one "big clump", under his chin. I knew he and I would not be lying down together any time soon.

Rasta Shoes

Rasta men do not have a specific type of shoes that they wear. Rasta men wear whatever is comfortable and suits their outfit. Back in the day if you were a true "roots man" you wore "Travel Fox." I don't think the Rasta man and roots men care to wear travel fox so much now a days, unless they are over age 50.

Rasta Clothing

Some Rasta men like to wear traditional African attire. Traditional African clothing is a little bit hard to find. I haven't checked online myself, but I'm sure online is a good place to start looking. Other than that, Rasta men wear main stream clothing. Usually with 1 or 2 Rasta accessories, like a Rasta belt or a Rasta Hat or maybe a Rasta backpack. There is no specific "Rasta clothing" for men.

Rasta Hats

Many Jamaican Rasta men like to wear leather Rasta hats. These hats are stylish and also called a crown, they hold long dreadlocks Rasta hair very well. Some

Rasta men prefer the knitted Rasta hats more for the reason of comfort. Some Rasta men do not wear Rasta hats at all and prefer to have their dreadlocks flowing out freely. This is a personal choice.

5 Reasons Rasta men cover their hair too

Some Rasta men cover their Dreadlocks too. It mostly depends on whether or not he is the type of Rasta who likes to keep his spiritual self-private.

Rasta men cover their hair....

As a way of being closer to Jah

To have a more "kingly" appearance while in public

To keep the holy dreadlocks clean and free of unwanted particles

To show respect to, and for, The Most High

To keep his locks sacred, private, and special **Myth buster:** Some people say a woman can only enter Rastafari thru her Rastafari man. This is complete rubbish! A woman can choose to follow the way of life of Rastafari on her own, and a woman can also be a born Rasta and never have a Rasta boyfriend or husband.

Empress Yuajah

Rasta Altar?

Some Rastafari have a "Rastafari Altar" in their home...The more "deep" one is holding the faith, the less the Altar he will use or, he may not even have one at all. That is because Rastafari comes from the heart.

How does Rasta use their Altar?

Some Rasta have a "Rastafari Altar" but it's not for prayer or sacrifice. It's mostly the place where you burn your Nag Champa Incense, or other Incense. You may also choose to smoke some Marijuana, and keep your ash tray there, or to light a scented candle to create a nice ambiance for relaxation and reflection.

A Rastafari Altar may also be where you might... I did say "might" keep a photo of King Selassie I. Some may call this an "Altar," but in Caribbean culture, its pretty much "a space" in your home where you keep your King Selassie I pictures, and your Lion of Judah Flag.

31

Rastafari Altar is personal Choice...

If having a Rastafari Altar helps one to embrace the faith, I say go for it! For me walking into my room and seeing the large "Lion of Judah" flag on my wall is enough. I can feel all the love, support, Royal presence of King Selassie I and Empress Menen... did I say love yet...? Right there in my room, so it is a personal choice.

Always Remember Rastafari is *NOT a religion* so having a "Rastafari Altar" is <u>not a requirement of the livity.</u>

Rastafari is an all-encompassing way of life that *focuses on how you live, how you think, how you treat other people, how you handle your body, and how you raise your children, what you do and do not allow into your home*....not rituals, ritualistic tools, nor ritualistic practices. **<u>Anybody that follows a "faith" of rituals is following Satan.</u>** Don't take my word for it, go and ask a Rastafari.

How to Build your Rastafari Altar

If you have just started following the faith, it's ok to have an "Altar" but after 9 months to 1 year you should get rid of it...! *Do what you are doing spiritually – sporadically!...and from your heart...*Your king Selassie I, Empress Menen, and Marcus Garvey photos should be strewn throughout every room in your home by that point any way. Yes Including in your Kitchen and in your Bathroom.

Your Rastafari Altar should be...a flat surface in your home containing...

Photo of King Selassie I
Incense holder
Scented Oil Burner
Rastafari "Lion of Judah" Flag
King James Version Bible
Ash tray for your "herb" or natural Tobacco
Important Literature of Rastafari, such as "the
Kebra Negast"

King Selassie I speeches
At least one Marcus Garvey Book
Book on African Truth and Culture such
as; "Blacked out through whitewash"

"Rastafari Altar" should be ...
Kept up high away from Children
Out of the way from visitors to interfere
with.

"Rastafari Altar" May also include...
Photo of Empress Menen, Nelson Mandela,
any other African leaders or Hero that you
admire...

Deep Rastafari and our Altar
You may choose to set up a "Rastafari Altar" in your home, however keep in mind that when holding the faith deep a *True Rastafari does not have an Altar,* all he does he does from the heart of his **holy temple (his body),** and in his palace(his entire home.)

His love of Jah, his feelings for the king, and His love of all things "Ital." etc. are available to him from his heart!

Set an Altar for burning your candles or your incense's, but it should not be used for prayer, or requests, or anything else because we as Rasta do not believe in that. A "Rastafari Altar" is simply a space in our home where we place our Rastafari spiritual Items.

The 10 Commandments

"And Jah spoke all these words, saying: 'I am the LORD your God...

ONE: 'You shall have no other Jahs before Me.'

TWO: 'You shall not make for yourself a carved image--and likeness of anything that is in Heaven above, or that is in the earth beneath, or that is in the water under the earth.'

THREE: 'You shall not take the name of the LORD your Jah in vain.'

FOUR: 'Remember the Sabbath day, to keep it holy.'

FIVE: 'Honor your father and your mother.'

SIX: 'You shall not murder.'

SEVEN: 'You shall not commit adultery.'

EIGHT: 'You shall not steal.'

NINE: 'You shall not bear false witness against your neighbor.'

TEN: 'You shall not covet your neighbor's house; you shall not covet your neighbor's wife, nor his male servant, nor his female servant, nor his ox, nor his donkey, nor anything that is your neighbor's.'

The 10 commandments are Jah laws, as imparted to his prophet and servant Moses.

"The Lion of Judah" Flag

The Lion of Judah Flag is represented by a Lion standing in a side view against 3 horizontal stripes of Red yellow and Green Stripes, and is also known as "The (old) Ethiopian Flag."

Red Yellow Green & Lion

The Lion of Judah flag is very important symbol in Rastafari Livity.

The color red represents the blood shed of the African peoples during slavery and colonization of the African Land.

The color yellow represents the Gold that was once part of the land but is no longer as the foreigners stole African riches.

The color Green symbolizes the abundance of lush greenery in Nature that exists all over the African land, and still abounds today.

The Lion Represents, King Selassie I himself.

All together...

The Lion of Judah (flag) represents...

The Black Ethiopian Royal Monarchy

The Lion of the Tribe of Judah (Haile Selassie I)

Victory

Love

Truth

Unity

Jah

Divinity

Strength

Royalty

As you can see, the reason Rasta like this flag so much is because its energy brings a blessing to the home.

Rasta desire the Lion of Judah Flag

Every Rasta owns or desires deeply to own, this very special, spiritual and beautiful African (Rastafari) Flag. This flag is the representation of Ras -Tafari spirituality as instructed by The Almighty Jah, "through" His Imperial Majesty, Emperor Haile Selassie I.

I own 5 of the 3 x5 feet Lion of Judah flags, and I am in love every time I look at them. Ras-Tafari!

Buy yours at www.jamaicanlove.org

"The Jamaican Flag"

The Jamaican Flag is depicted by a large yellow "X" and 4 triangles filling in the four triangular spaces surrounding to the yellow "X."

"Big Yellow X" black and Green

I figured I would let you in on a little secret. When embracing the faith you should know the Jamaican flag holds almost as much weight as the Rastafari Lion Judah Flag. The reason...? Jamaica is a very important part of Rastafari Culture.

Bob Marley was born in 9 Mile Saint Ann parish, Jamaica

King Selassie I visited Jamaica in 1966

Both Mortimer Planno and Howell Percival (The first Rasta man) were born in Jamaica

Marcus Garvey was born in St. Ann's Bay, Jamaica

Therefor Rastafari and Jamaican Culture are one.

The Yellow X Represents the Strength of the Jamaican people.

I like to see the "X" as two crossed arms with clenched fists, breaking the Shackles and chains of Bondage/Slavery.

The color Green represents the abundance of lush Green nature of the Land

The color Black represents the beautiful black people of Jamaica.

Give thanks to the Most High, Jah...Rastafari.

Many Rastafari have both 1 Lion of Judah flag and 1 Jamaican flag. These flags symbolize the everlasting love and Covenant All Rasta has with Jah the Almighty Creator. They have a *powerful meaning* of love and unity and strength when you hang them side by side in the home.

Sabbath & Holy Days

For those of you who do not know, Rastafari do keep a Sabbath on which we fast once a week (Saturday.) Here is more about the Covenant with Jah and the Holy Sabbath of Rastafari from the Christian Bible.

<u>Numbers 15:32-36</u>

"...**12**And the LORD spake unto Moses, saying, **13**Speak thou also unto the children of Israel, saying, Verily my sabbaths ye shall keep: for it is a sign between me and you throughout your generations; that ye may know that I am the LORD that doth sanctify you. **14**Ye shall keep the sabbath therefore; for it is holy unto you: every one that defileth it shall surely be put to death: for whosoever doeth any work therein, that soul shall be cut off from among his people...

<u>15</u>Six days may work be done; but in the seventh is the sabbath of rest, holy to

the LORD: whosoever doeth any work in the sabbath day, he shall surely be put to death. 16Wherefore the children of Israel shall keep the sabbath, to observe the sabbath throughout their generations, for a perpetual covenant. 17It is a sign between me and the children of Israel for ever: for in six days the LORD made Zion and earth, and on the seventh day he rested, and was refreshed..." To learn more of a deeper explanation about Rastafari and our Sabbath Read "Rastafari Spirituality for African Americans."*

Holy Days

The Nyahbinghi Order in Jamaica celebrates for 7 days and nights the following events:

- 7 January Ethiopian Nativity of Christ
- 2l April Visit of H.I.M. to Jamaica 1966
- 25 May All African Liberation Day

- 23 July Birth of HAILE SELASSIE I 1892
- 11 September Ethiopian New Year
- 2 November H.LM. Coronation 1930

Spiritual/African Re-education....

It is a good Idea as a new Rasta, to begin to learn the Truth about Africans and our contributions globally. I have included 10 black inventions for you in his book, and some information on the first Rastafari man.

10 Cool Black Inventions!

A very important part of the Rastafari Livity is to know your history and to take pride in which you are. You will not feel very proud, if the only accomplishments you are aware of are contributions and successes by other nations. Here is a list of *10 Great black inventors and their inventions....*

mk1. The Traffic Signal!
Garrett Augustus Morgan

The son of former slaves, Garett Morgan was born in 1877 in Kentucky. He later moved to Cincinnati and then Cleveland, where he owned and operated a sewing-machine repair business and earned quite a

46

reputation as a technician. A multi-talented businessman. Before The invention of the Traffic Signal by Mr. there were lots of accidents involving motor vehicles. Mr. Morgan felt compelled to create a device that would prevent such situations. The Traffic signal was pattented on November 23 1923. The rights to his invention to General Electric. Isn't that amazing. (Red Yellow and Green) Ras Tafari

and

The Gas Mask

But Morgan's most prolific accomplishments came in his role as an inventor. He received a patent for the first gas mask invention in 1914, but it wasn't until two years later that the idea really took off. When a group of workers got stuck in a tunnel below Lake Erie after an explosion, Morgan and a team of men donned the masks to help get them out. After the rescue was a success, requests for the masks began pouring in.

2. The Lawn Sprinkler & The portable Ironing Board

Elijah McCoy

Elijah McCoy (1844-1929), was born in Colchester, Ontario, on May 2, 1844. His mother and father were George and Emillia McCoy. They were slaves from Kentucky who escaped through the Underground Railroad. Elijah McCoy invented the portable ironing board, rubber shoe heels, tire tread, and lawn sprinkler, to name a few. Many inventors tried to sell imitations of the devices that Elijah invented, but companies wanted the real items, that's how the term "the real McCoy" came to be.

3. The First Clock
Benjamin Banneker

Benjamin Banneker, born November 9, 1731, created the first Clock. Apparently using as a pocket watch as a model, Banneker carved wooden replicas of each piece and used the parts to make a clock that struck hourly. He completed the clock in 1753, at the age of 22. The clock continued to work until his death.

4. 3D Glasses
Kenneth Dunkley

Kenneth Dunkley earned a significant place in the history of black inventors by creating Three Dimensional Viewing Glasses (3-DVG). This patented invention ...Born in Karsalona, New Mexico and was born in December 12,1966.He is still living today and is the president of Holospace Labarotories Inc. in Camp Hill,Pennsylvania.

5. *Home security inventions*
Marie Van Brittan Brown

While home security systems today are more advanced than ever, back in 1966 the idea for a home surveillance device seemed almost unthinkable. That was the year famous African-American inventor Marie Van Brittan Brown, and her partner Albert Brown, applied for an invention patent for a closed-circuit television security system – the forerunner to the modern home security system.

Brown's system had a set of four peep holes and a camera that could slide up and down to look out each one. Anything the camera picked up would appear on a monitor. An additional feature of Brown's invention was that a person also could unlock a door with a remote control.

A female black inventor far ahead of her time, Marie Van Brittan Brown created an invention that was the first in a long string of home-security inventions that continue to flood the market today.

6. Potato Chips
George Crum

Every time a person crunches into a potato chip, he or she is enjoying the delicious taste of one of the world's most famous snacks – a treat that might not exist without the contribution of black inventor George Crum.

The son of an African-American father and a Native American mother, Crum was working as the chef in the summer of 1853 when he incidentally invented the chip. It all began when a patron who ordered a plate of French-fried potatoes sent them back to Crum's kitchen because he felt they were too thick and soft.

To teach the picky patron a lesson, Crum sliced a new batch of potatoes as thin as he possibly could, and then fried them until they were hard and crunchy. Finally, to top them off, he added a generous heaping of salt. To Crum's surprise, the dish ended up being a hit with the patron and a new snack was born!

Years later, Crum opened his own restaurant that had a basket of potato chips on every table. Though Crum never attempted to patent his invention, the snack was eventually mass-produced and sold in bags – providing thousands of jobs nationwide.

7. The Blood Bank
Dr.Charles Drew

It's impossible to determine how many hundreds of thousands of people would have lost their lives without the contributions of African-American inventor Dr. Charles Drew. This physician, researcher and surgeon revolutionized the understanding of blood plasma – leading to the invention of blood banks.

Born in 1904 in Washington, D.C., Charles Drew excelled from early on in both intellectual and athletic pursuits. After becoming a doctor and working as a college instructor, Drew went to Columbia University to do his Ph.D. on blood storage. He completed a thesis titled Banked Blood that invented a method of separating and storing plasma, allowing it to be dehydrated for later use. It was the first time Columbia awarded a doctorate to an African-American.

At the onset of World War II, Drew was called upon to put his techniques into practice. He emerged as the leading authority on mass transfusion and processing methods, and went on to helm the American Red Cross blood bank. When the Armed Forces ordered that only Caucasian blood be given to soldiers, Drew protested and resigned.

9. The Super Soaker
Lonnie G. Johnson

An anonymous source said of the Super Soaker®: "I got fired from a job once because of my Super Soaker. I guess that's what happens when you accidentally drench a customer when you're trying to get a co-worker who ducks."

Famous black inventor and scientist Lonnie G. Johnson probably didn't have that little scenario in mind when he invented the Super Soaker squirt gun, but it is one of the countless memories that can be recalled by those who were young enough to enjoy the Super Soaker after its release in 1989.

Johnson's resume boasts work with the US Air Force and NASA (including work on the Galileo Jupiter probe and Mars Observer project), a nomination for astronaut training and more than 40 patents, but it's for a squirt gun that he's best known. Johnson conceived of a novelty water gun powered by air pressure in 1982 when he conducted an experiment at home on a heat pump that used water instead of Freon. This experimentation, which resulted in Johnson shooting a stream of water across his bathroom into the tub, led directly to the development of the Power Drencher, the precursor to the Super Soaker.

Lonnie G. Johnson now has his own company, Johnson Research and Development, and continues to do work for NASA.

9. Long Distance Cargo Refrigeration System

Fredrick McKinley

Anytime you see a truck on the highway transporting refrigerated or frozen food, you're seeing the work of Frederick McKinley Jones.

One of the most prolific Black inventors ever, Jones patented more than 60 inventions in his lifetime. While more than 40 of those patents were in the field of refrigeration, Jones is most famous for inventing an automatic refrigeration system for long haul trucks and railroad cars.

Before Jones' invention, the only way to keep food cool in trucks was to load them with ice. Jones was inspired to invent the system after talking with a truck driver who lost his whole cargo of chicken because he couldn't reach his destination before the ice melted. As a solution, the African-American inventor developed a roof-mounted cooling system to make sure food stayed fresh.

In addition to that refrigerator invention, Jones also invented an air-conditioning unit for military field hospitals, a refrigerator for military field kitchens, a self-starting gas engine, a series of devices for movie projectors and box-office equipment that gave tickets and made change. Jones was posthumously awarded the National Medal of Technology in 1991 – the first Black inventor to ever receive such an honor.

10. First Open Heart Surgery
Dale Hale Williams

Daniel Hale Williams was born on January 18, 1856 in Hollidaysburg, Pennsylvania. He was the fifth of seven children born to Daniel and Sarah Williams. Daniel's father was a barber and moved the family to Annapolis, Maryland but died shortly thereafter of tuberculosis. Daniel's mother realized she could not manage the entire family and sent some of the children to live with relatives. Daniel was apprenticed to a shoemaker in Baltimore but ran away to join his mother who had moved to Rockford, Illinois. He later moved to Edgerton, Wisconsin where he joined his sister and opened his own barber shop. After moving to nearby Janesville, Daniel became fascinated with a local physician and decided to follow his path. He began working as an apprentice to the physician (Dr. Henry Palmer) for two years and in 1880 entered what is now known as Northwestern University Medical School. After graduation from Northwestern in 1883, he opened his own medical office in Chicago, Illinois.

Because of primitive social and medical circumstances existing in that era, much of Williams early medical practice called for him to treat patients in their homes, including conducting occasional surgeries on kitchen tables. In doing so, Williams utilized many of the emerging antiseptic, sterilization procedures of the day and thereby gained a reputation for professionalism. He was soon appointed as a surgeon on the staff of the South Side Dispensary and then a clinical instructor in anatomy at Northwestern. In 1889 he was appointed to the Illinois State Board of Health and one year later set for to create an interracial hospital.

On January 23, 1891 Daniel Hale Williams established the Provident Hospital and Training School Association, a three story building which held 12 beds and served members of the community as a whole.

The school also served to train Black nurses and utilized doctors of all races. Within its first year, 189 patients were treated at Provident Hospital and of those 141 saw a complete recovery, 23 had recovered significantly, three had seen change in their condition and 22 had died. For a brand new hospital, at that time, to see an 87% success rate was phenomenal considering the financial and health conditions of the patient, and primitive conditions of most hospitals. Much can be attributed to Williams insistence on the highest standards concerning procedures and sanitary conditions.

Two and a half years later, on July 9, 1893, a young Black man named James Cornish was injured in a bar fight, stabbed in the chest with a knife. By the time he was transported to Provident Hospital he was seeking closer and closer to death, having lost a great deal of blood and having gone into shock. Williams was faced with the choice of opening the man's chest and possibly operating internally when that was almost unheard of in that day in age. Internal operations were unheard of because any entrance into the chest or abdomen of a patient would almost surely bring with it resulting infection and therefore death. Williams made the decision to operate and opened the man's chest. He saw the damage to the man's pericardium (sac surrounding the heart) and sutured it, then applied antiseptic procedures before closing his chest. Fifty one days later, James Cornish walked out of Provident Hospital completely recovered

and would go on to live for another fifty
years. Unfortunately, Williams was so busy
with other matters, he did not bother to
document the event and others made
claims to have first achieved the feat of
performing open heart surgery.
Fortunately, local newspapers of the day
did spread the news and Williams received
the acclaim he deserved. It should be noted
however that while he is known as the first
person to perform an open heart surgery, it
is actually more noteworthy that he was
the first surgeon to open the chest cavity
successfully without the patient dying of
infection. His procedures would therefore
be used as standards for future internal
surgeries.

The Ethnicity of the Israelites

Ham was one of Noah's three sons; Shem and Japheth were the other two. Noah's descendants repopulated the earth after the Great Flood. Ham's descendants are traced to the families of Africa. <u>Ham (Khawm) in Hebrew means BLACK, HOT AND BURNT</u>.
Ham had four sons,

1. CUSH (Ethiopians / Cushites & Nubians),
2. MIZRAIM (Egyptians / Khemet),
3. PHUT (Ancient Libyans or Somalia),
4. CANAAN (Canaanite, the original inhabitants of the land of Israel) genesis 10:6-19.

All four of Ham's sons and their descendants settled in and around the continent of Africa, this includes the so called Middle East which is also a part of the Continent of Africa. Ham sons are the people of the African continent, the Ancient Egyptians, Ethiopians, Somalia's, Canaanites etc.

The Israelites are descendants of Noah son
SHEM, through Abraham, he is the father of
the Hebrew Israelite Nation. Abraham is
the father of Isaac, Isaac is the father of
Jacob, Jacob had twelve sons and these sons
are the progenitors of the Israelite nation.
The Twelve tribes of Israel are as follows:

REUBEN
 GAD
SIMEON
 ASHER
LEVI
 NAPHILTI
JUDAH
 ISSACHAR
ZEBULON
 JOSEPH
DAN
 BENJAMIN

each one of Jacob's sons became a tribal
nation that made up the greater nation of
Israel. EXAMPLE: Reuben's descendants
became known as the tribe of Reuben.
Judah's descendants became known as the
tribe of Judah and so on and so forth. The

nation of Israel is the descendants of Jacob who had his name changed to Israel by the Most High (Gen 28:32). That's the basics, let's move on to the meat of our lesson.

We will begin with the story of Jacob's second Youngest son Joseph, and his time in Egypt. Joseph was one of the twelve sons of Jacob (Yaqob in Hebrew). Jacob sired Joseph in his old age, and he was clearly his favorite son. This caused Joseph's brothers to become jealous of him.

Ultimately, their jealousy resulted in Joseph being sold by Arab merchants as a slave to Egyptians.

Over the course of time Joseph became Viceroy (Governor) of Egypt and was second in command to Pharaoh in authority. There was a famine in Canaan, where Jacob and his sons lived. (Pharaoh had a dream which Joseph interpreted. His dream told of the forthcoming famine and gave Egypt an opportunity to prepare by storing food.) So, Jacob sent his ten sons to Egypt to buy bread. When Joseph's ten brothers came into Egypt they were brought before him. Joseph recognized his brothers, but they didn't recognize him (Genesis 42:1-8).

Since the biblical Egyptians were a black-skinned people, Joseph had to be black-skinned also. If he were white skinned, his brothers would have recognized him easily among the "black" Egyptians. His brothers thought Joseph was another Egyptian.

The ancient Egyptians of Joseph time were indeed what we know today as "black", this is a fact attested to by many.

Gerald Massey, English writer and author of the book, Egypt the Light of the World, wrote, **"The dignity is so ancient that the insignia of the Pharaoh evidently belonged to the time when Egyptians wore nothing but the girdle of the Negro." (p 251)**
Sir Richard Francis Burton, a 19th century English explorer, writer and linguist in 1883 wrote to Gerald Massey, **"You are quite right about the "AFRICAN" origin of the**

Egyptians. I have 100 human skulls to prove it."

Scientist, R. T. Prittchett, states in his book The Natural History of Man, **"In their complex and many of the complexions and in physical peculiarities the Egyptians were an "AFRICAN" race (p 124-125).**

The Ancient Greek historian Herodotus, who visited Egypt in the 5th century B.C.E., saw the Egyptians face to face and described them as black-skinned with woolly hair.

Anthropologist, Count Constatin de Volney (1727-1820), spoke about the race of the Egyptians that produced the Pharaohs. He later paid tribute to Herodotus' discovery when he said:

The ancient Egyptians were true Negroes of the same type as all native born Africans. That being so, we can see how their blood mixed for several centuries with that of the Romans and Greeks, must have lost the intensity of its original

color, while retaining none the less the imprint of its original mold. We can even state as a general principle that the face (referring to The Sphinx) is a kind of monument able, in many cases, to attest to or shed light on historical evidence on the origins of the people."

The fact that the ancient Egyptians were black-skin prompted Volney to make the following statement:

"What a subject for meditation, just think that the race of black men today our slaves and the object of our scorn, is the very race to which we owe our arts, science and even the use of our speech."

Read the Rest of the article or visit the following URL

http://www.angelfire.com/ill/hebrewisrael/printpages/phys.html

Religion vs. Rastafari, for Africans?

Christianity, Buddhism, Judaism, Hinduism, Catholicism are great Religions, But only *The Ras Tafari way of life,* promotes the *Natural Beauty and "upliftment" of the Black hue-man being.* We as Black hue-mans have our own....

Economical
Spiritual
Dietary
Familial
Social
...Needs!

Rastafari is the proper choice to cater to the spiritual needs of the black man, black woman and black child, and black family as a whole, of which not any "Religion" does not address.

The Black hue-man and Religion

There is no reason why a Black skinned coily haired hue-man today, American, Jamaican, Canadian, African, or otherwise,

should choose to follow a "Religion."
Religion may be and is detrimental to the
Black Hue-man in the following ways....

Feelings of Inadequacy: Religion may
cause the black hue-man to feel inadequate
in comparison to *others who are of the same
ethnic origin* as his Religious
Messiah/Prophet.

Low in Self Esteem: Religion may cause
the black hue-man to become low in self-
esteem as *his appearance does not resemble
the appearance of his religious God.* He may
silently be telling himself, "My people are
ugly", in regards to his own black African
Appearance, and believe that he is
unworthy of Respect, Success and Love.

Hopeless about life: Religion may cause
the black - hue-man to feel hopeless about
life, as he dedicates himself to a religion
that, acknowledges not his people, nor his
culture, nor his black identity, nor his
history, nor the positive contributions of
his own black ancestors. With the

exception of referring to black people as "slaves."

Black people worshiping depictions of Caucasians...

A very wise Rastafari friend of mine, from England says..."*The Chinese worship their "Chinese God," The white man worships a "White God," and the Indians have their "Indian God...." Black people are the only ones who worship a God that does not resemble their own appearance!" (– We can thank slavery for this...)*

Black People are Royals in Rastafari!

The Rastafari way of life is the best choice for the black hue-man who wants to embrace a spirituality of truth, and that promotes his own image identity and Culture.

Rastafari encourages black people to see themselves as "Kings and Queens" of the earth, also known as "Kingman and Empress." This type of thinking encourages the black hue-man to live a life that is "Royal" and clean, the way Jah intended.

Jah

*"...Sing unto God, sing praises to his name:
extol him that rideth upon the Heavens by
his name **JAH**, and rejoice before him."*
– Psalms 68 vs. 4 King James Version

Jah is "the God" of the Universe

Jah is the God of the Universe. There is only one God just as there is only one Universe. "God" does not exist. Only Jah!

The image of Jah

The image (vibration) or "spiritual form" of Jah is...
African,
Black,
Powerful,
Natty (Dreadlocks)

Jah is a spiritual "Storehouse" of "Blackness"

All things that exist here on earth have a spiritual existence or "storehouse" depending on how you see it.

All living things before becoming physical are in spiritual form. Jah also has a spiritual store house, or is a spiritual store house depending on how you see it. If he wants to take physical form he can, and sometimes he does in a manner of speaking. But Jah has one true image or "likeness" if he were to take physical form... If you could see him... you would see that he is in fact **African, black, and Natty!** <u>Give thanks and praises unto The Most High, Jah Rastafari.</u>

5 Biblical Covenants of Jah

1. Jah's Covenant With Noah

Centuries before the time of Abraham, Jah made a covenant with <u>Noah</u>, assuring Noah that He would never again destroy the world by flood (Gen. 9).

Noah lived at a time when the whole earth was filled with violence and corruption -- yet Noah did not allow the evil standards of his day to rob him of fellowship with Jah. He stood out as the only one who "walked with Jah" (<u>Gen. 6:9</u>), as was also true of his great-grandfather Enoch (<u>Gen. 5:22</u>). "Noah was a just man, perfect in his generations" (<u>Gen. 6:9</u>). The Lord singled out Noah from among all his contemporaries and chose him as the man to accomplish a great work.

When Jah saw the wickedness that prevailed in the world (<u>Gen. 6:5</u>), He told Noah of His intention to destroy the ancient world by a universal flood. Jah instructed Noah to build an ark (a large barge) in which he and his family would survive the universal deluge. Noah believed Jah and "according to all that Jah commanded him, so he did" (Gen. 6:22).

Noah is listed among the heroes of faith. "By faith Noah, being divinely warned of things not yet seen, moved with Jahly fear, prepared an ark for the saving of his household, by which he condemned the world and became heir of the righteousness which is according to faith" (Heb. 11:7).

With steadfast confidence in Jah, Noah started building the ark. During this time, Noah continued to preach Jah's judgment and mercy, warning the unJahly of their approaching doom. Peter reminds us of how Jah "did not spare the ancient world, but saved Noah, one of eight people, a preacher of righteousness, bringing in the flood on the world of the unJahly" (2 Pet. 2:5).

Noah preached for 120 years, apparently without any converts. At the end of that time, "when ... the longsuffering of Jah waited in the days of Noah ... eight souls were saved through water" (1 Pet. 3:20).

People continued in their evil ways and ignored his pleadings and warnings until the flood overtook them. When the ark was ready, Noah entered in with all kinds of animals "and the Lord shut him in" (Gen. 7:16), cut off completely from the rest of mankind.

Noah was grateful to the Lord who had delivered him from the flood. After the flood, he built an altar to Jah (Gen. 8:20) and made a sacrifice, which was accepted graciously, for in it "the Lord smelled a soothing aroma" (Gen. 8:21).

The Lord promised Noah and his descendants that He would never destroy the world again with a universal flood (Gen. 9:15). The Lord made an everlasting covenant with Noah and his descendants, establishing the rainbow as the sign of His promise (Gen. 9:1-17).

Another part of the covenant involved the sanctity of human life, i.e., that "whoever sheds man's blood, by man his blood shall be shed; for in the image of Jah He made man" (Gen. 9:6). Every time we see a rainbow today we are reminded of that agreement -- this covenant has not been done away with. As long as Jah still sends rainbows after a storm, capital punishment will still be a part of Jah's law for the human race.

2. Jah's Covenant With Abraham

In making a covenant with Abraham, Jah promised to bless his descendants and make them His own special people -- in return, Abraham was to remain faithful to Jah and to serve as a channel through which Jah's blessings could flow to the rest of the world (Gen. 12:1-3).

Abraham's story begins with his passage with the rest of his family from Ur of the Chaldeans in ancient southern Babylonia (Gen. 11:31). He and his family moved north along the trade routes of the ancient world and settled in the prosperous trade center of Haran, several hundred miles to the northwest.

While living in Haran, at the age of 75, Abraham received a call from Jah to go to a strange, unknown land that Jah would show him. The Lord promised Abraham that He would make him and his descendants a great nation (Gen. 12:1-3). The promise must have seemed unbelievable to Abraham because his wife Sarah was childless (Gen. 11:30-31; 17:15). Abraham obeyed Jah with no hint of doubt or disbelief.

Abraham took his wife and his nephew, Lot, and went toward the land that Jah would show him. Abraham moved south along the trade routes from Haran, through Shechem and Bethel, to the land of Canaan. Canaan was a populated area at the time, inhabited by the war-like Canaanites; so, Abraham's belief that Jah would ultimately give this land to him and his descendants was an act of faith.

The circumstances seemed quite difficult, but Abraham's faith in Jah's promises allowed him to trust in the Lord. In Genesis 15, the Lord reaffirmed His promise to Abraham. The relationship between Jah and Abraham should be understood as a covenant relationship -- the most common form of arrangement between individuals in the ancient world. In this case, Abraham agreed to go to the land that Jah would show him (an act of faith on his part), and Jah agreed to make Abraham a great nation (Gen. 12:1-3).

In Genesis 15 Abraham became anxious about the promise of a nation being found in his descendants because of his advanced age -- and the Lord then reaffirmed the earlier covenant. A common practice of that time among heirless families was to adopt a slave who would inherit the master's goods. Therefore, because Abraham was childless, he proposed to make a slave, Eliezer of Damascus, his heir (Gen. 15:2). But Jah rejected this action and challenged Abraham's faith: "'Look now toward Zion, and count the stars if you are able to number them.' And He said to him, 'So shall your descendants be'" (Gen. 15:5).

Abraham's response is the model of believing faith: "And he believed in the Lord, and He accounted it to him for righteousness" (Gen. 15:6). The rest of Genesis 15 consists of a ceremony between Abraham and Jah that was commonly used in the ancient world to formalize a covenant (Gen. 15:7-21). Jah repeated this covenant to Abraham' son, Isaac (Gen. 17:19). Stephen summarized the story in the book of Acts 7:1-8.

2. The Mosaic Covenant

The Israelites moved to Egypt during the time of Joseph. A new Pharaoh came upon the scene and turned the Israelites into common slaves. The people cried out to the Jah of their forefathers. "So Jah heard their groaning, and Jah remembered His covenant with Abraham, with Isaac, and with Jacob" (Exo. 2:24). After a series of ten plagues upon the land of Egypt, Jah brought the Israelites out "of Egypt with great power and with a mighty hand" (Exo. 32:11).

Three months after leaving the land of Egypt, the children of Israel camped at the base of Mount Sinai (Exo. 19:1). Jah promised to make a covenant with the Israelites (Exo. 19:3-6). Before they even knew the conditions of the contract, the people agreed to abide by whatever Jah said (Exo. 19:8).

This covenant was between Jah and the people of Israel -- you and I are not a party in this contract (and never have been). The Ten Commandments are the foundation of the covenant, but they are not the entirety of it.

After giving the first ten commands, the people asked the Lord to speak no more (Exo. 20:18-20). Moses then drew near to the presence of Jah to hear the rest of the covenant (Exo. 20:21). After receiving the Law, Moses spoke the words of the covenant to all of the people, and the people agreed to obey (Exo. 24:4).

Moses then wrote the conditions of the covenant down, offered sacrifices to Jah, and then sprinkled both the book and the people with blood to seal the covenant (Exo. 24:8). This covenant between Jah and the people of Israel was temporary -- Jah promised a day when He would make a new covenant, not only with Israel but also with all mankind. "Behold, the days are coming, says the Lord, when I will make a new covenant with the house of Israel and with the house of Judah -- not according to the covenant that I made with their fathers in the day that I took them by the hand to lead them out of the land of Egypt, My covenant which they broke, though I was a husband to them, says the Lord. *But this is the covenant that I will make with the house of Israel after those days, says the Lord: I will put My law in their minds, and write it on their hearts; and I will be their God,* (This is Rastafari) and they shall be My people" (Jer. 31:31-34).

4. Jah's Covenant with David

Another covenant was between Jah and King David, in which David and his descendants were established as the royal heirs to the throne of the nation of Israel (2 Sam. 7:12-13).

This covenant agreement reached its fulfillment when Jesus, a descendant of the line of David, was born in Bethlehem. The gospel of Matthew starts off by showing Christ was "the Son of David" (Matt. 1:1), and thus He had the right to rule over Jah's people. Peter preached that Jesus Christ was a fulfillment of Jah's promise to David (Acts 2:29-36).

5. The Covenant Of Christ

The New Testament makes a clear distinction between the covenants of the Mosaic Law and the covenant of Promise. The apostle Paul spoke of these "two covenants," one originating "from Mount Sinai," the other from "the Jerusalem above" (Gal. 4:24-26). Paul also argued that the covenant established at Mount Sinai was a "ministry of death" and "condemnation" (2 Cor. 3:7, 9).

The death of Christ ushered in the new covenant under which we are justified by Jah's grace and mercy -- it is now possible to have the true forgiveness of sins. Jesus Himself is the Mediator of this better covenant between Jah and man (Heb. 9:15). Jesus' sacrificial death served as the oath, or pledge, which Jah made to us to seal this new covenant.

The "new covenant" is the new agreement Jah has made with mankind, based on the death and resurrection of Jesus Christ. The concept of a new covenant originated with the promise of Jeremiah that Jah would accomplish for His people what the old covenant had failed to do (Jer.

31:31-34; Heb. 11:7-13). Under this new covenant, Jah would write His Law on human hearts.

When Jesus ate the Passover meal at the Last Supper with His disciples, He spoke of the cup and said, "this is My blood of the new covenant, which is shed for many for the remission of sins" (Matt. 26:28). Luke's account refers to this cup as symbolizing "the new covenant in My blood, which is shed for you" (Luke 22:20).

When Paul recited the account he had received concerning the Last Supper, he quoted these words of Jesus about the cup as "the new covenant in My blood" (1 Cor.

16 Principles of Rastafari

Rastafari was...

Created and implemented by Jah in the heart of every Rasta man Rasta women and Rasta child to....

1.   *Help and heal, the black nation out of Slavery, into <u>freedom and independence</u> ...*

2.   *Teach the black nation how to live peaceably and neighboring with surrounding Nations...*

3.   *Guide the black nation to live clean, pure and holy in order that we may Enter Zion.*

When you read the following Rastafari Principles with this overstanding ...then you begin acquire the *"Spiritual Essence"* of what it means to live as Rasta.

Categorical Breakdown

I have separated the Rastafari Principles into *3 major Categories,* for "Overstanding" and Organization.

Self
Zion
"Others"

Self

The Rastafari Principles "Self" refer to the self and the body as holy temple...

Zion

The Rastafari principles "Zion" refer to our day to day living (Zion living...)

Others

The Rastafari Principles of "Others" refer to living amongst and working with peoples of other nations, and living and working within the black nation...

Self

"...Do you not know that you are God's temple and that God's Spirit dwells in you..?."
- **1 Corinthians 3:16**

1.Keep the Temple Clean

In Rastafari the Body is also known as "The Temple." It is very easy to "defile" The Temple, with many "unclean" habits, behaviors, and foods. Rasta keep The Temple clean and Holy so that we may be deemed "fit" to enter Zion, in which only the "clean" are welcome.

Temple as "Holy House"

Your temple/body is also a "house of Jah." Your body is used for prayer fasting and Jah dwells inside your holy house with you so that you can always be with him.

As Rastafari we adhere to a strict diet of "clean" fruits, vegetables, and herbs in order that we keep the temple as "holy" and as clean possible. Rastafari also do a once a month detoxification to clean out build up that may be in our digestive system. As Rasta "clean" means, body, mind, and spirit.

More tips to keep the mind body spirit clean

"Body Cleanliness"

No smoking of Babylon cigarettes;
Rastafari smoke natural marijuana or
natural tobacco
No ingesting of Babylon pharmaceuticals
No eating fast food
No eating meat

"Mind Cleanliness"
No horror movies
No conversations of corruption (gossip)
No porn movies or photos
No corrupted talk shows like Jerry
Springer

"Spirit Cleanliness"

Keep Jah 10 Commandments
Do Good unto others
Be the first to Apologize
Avoid Arguments and disagreements

2.Eat not of Flesh

As Rasta we believe to eat meat is to eat "dead Flesh" For some this is their way of life and no disrespect to anybody who does that. For the sake of Rastafari, and the will and power of the Almighty Jah, *Rasta do not eat meat!*

Here are some very clear distinct reasons for this principle.

Medical history of animal unknown
Did you know meat has to <u>rot</u> in the body before it can exit the body?

Maintaining a body that is meat free more spiritually aligned
Meat eating may disrupt or clog up communications with Angels and Ancestors

Rasta do not eat meat, we care very much about our spiritual connections with our Ancestors and Angles. Anybody who tells you Rasta eat meat...its not true we do not! If someone does this and calls themself

"Rasta" this is not the sprit of Jah they are dealing with.

3.Self-Reliance

Self-Reliance in Rastafari means making your own money. To be living off the earnings of another may be considered a sin unless the two of you are married or common law. As Rasta we know we must make our own individual contribution to society, so that we can hold our head up high and appreciate the things that we have, and have earned.

Self-Reliance, Anti-Crime

Rastafari do not believe in a life of crime, or breaking the law in any way such as stealing, or lying, for money. Therefor however one embraces this faith and chooses to generate money, it must be clean and honest to be considered of Jah-Rastafari.

4. Servant of Jah

This principle which applies to the self is to help those who follow Rastafari to understand that to be a Servant of Jah is of the highest honour to self.

How can we become Servants of Jah?

Humble ourselves in Adversity
Encourage others to embrace Rastafari
(no there is no Reward in Zion for doing so)
Bring "More Love" and Unity, to the any situation
Live for Jah not for our ego, and not for Babylon
Help those in need without being asked
Feed the poor

Rasta knows Jah needs more soldiers of love in Babylon. Be a beacon of light and love for someone else. Be a model of love and Jah "Highness" to others at all times.

I work for Jah!

I always have it in the back of my mind...no matter what I am doing, that I must always remember who I represent...Jah! I never want someone to say "I knew a Rasta girl...and..." then have something negative to follow it up with. So I try to be positive, and remember who I work for.

5. Self-Awareness

Self-awareness leads to self Esteem.

Many Black youth and adults struggle with their self-Awareness, due to a lack of information about our history and culture, and brainwashing, in school and media about the black identity. These things cause us to struggle with our self-esteem.

Self (Awareness) Esteem for black people

Natural black hair

Anybody who wants to follow Rastafari as a way of life, must wear their hair in natural beautiful dreadlocks. Doing this will help to build your self-esteem tenfold. I know because I have my hair in locks, and I am more beautiful and free, now then when I was wearing wigs, weaves and extensions. If you are not ready to lock, be sure to embrace your natural coily hair as an afro.

Shop Black

Supporting black business is extremely important for Self Esteem and the Rastafari community. This builds black business, and creates self-esteem by shopping in a shop that has your image and interests, and identity, and health in mind. Too much black hue-mans are shopping in stores, that know nothing of our culture, and physical or spiritual needs. Support black business and also black Authors, and as a black hue-man, you may feel more "spiritually attuned and grounded."

Positive Black Vocabulary

It's time we as black hue-man's start to use "positive vocabulary" when making references to our coily African black hair and black skin complexion.

In Reference to our hair we may say...

Jah hair

Coily hair

Royal Crown

Wooly Jesus hair

In reference to our beautiful skin tone we may say:

High Melanin Complexion

Jah skin

Honorable Completion
Royal Complexion
Beautiful African Skin
Burnt Brass Color
Using these "terms" will go a long way to creating self-love, and inner self esteem as a black hue-man. I was sent here to tell you this.

Self-awareness for other nations

Self-Awareness as Rastafari is knowing and learning about and accepting your own culture, roots and identity.

You can do this by doing some Google searches, reading books, on your culture and peoples, and by asking questions of the Elders In your family.

Self-Awareness is a very important Rastafari Principles because as we know much of the Culture of the African Nation was lost due to slavery. Many black people today are disconnected from their roots. Jah wants all people of all creeds to know

97

their roots and where they come from and Know who they are.

6. Freedom of Self
Freedom of Self as Rastafari means...
Freedom to choose our own spiritual destiny

This means freedom to believe in and to practice whatever faith or culture we choose, or belong to.

Freedom to express and create

This means freedom to share our ideas and creations with the world via art, music, poetry, etc.

Freedom to "Roam"

Freedom to "Roam" means if we choose to simply roam the earth, without doing anything that Babylon asks of us, we should be able to do it. Animals do it...they live free, they roam, just the way Jah intended them to do....Why not people too....if we choose to do so?

Others

"...Do nothing from rivalry or conceit, but in humility count others more significant than yourselves..." - Philippians 2:3

7.Unity

Jah never wanted people to disrespect each other and fight over land, or "Race," or Culture etc. But, Rather Jah wanted all nations to unite as one under his name, and to show Respect and love, as fellow nations.

Jah knows we can all share this land, respect each other's culture and live in peace. Man's mind of greed and power has made this nearly impossible.

Unity with Other Nations

As Rastafari unity with others means that we must never see ourselves as less than or greater than another human being. Rasta views other people and other nations, as all connected to each other and all drawing life from the same force – Jah!

Unity with others as Rastafari means....

"Living peaceably, and neighbouringly alongside and with other nations."

Rastafari see those of other Cultures and nations as our brothers and our sisters under the name of the creator of all things - *Jah.*

"Inity" – The unity within

Rastarfari Unity within, is also known as "Inity" and means to unite the physical self with the spiritual self. Life is much more rewarding, when we encourage and love our "spirit self" and allow it expression, and emergence into our physical existence. life.

In Rastafari Unity within also means **Acceptance** of who you are without, as well as within. Without "unity within" there shall be no unity without.

How to Practice Unity within

To practice unity within, we simply exercise our spirit self. Do this by

Paining

Song writing
Writing a book
Meditation
Singing
Anything that is creative/exercises our spirit, generates unity within.

Unity with the Black Nation

Unity with the black nation is *one of the most important principles of embracing Rastafari as a faith.* Again Rastafari was implemented by Jah to help heal the black nation. Jah say "all Rasta, must have a deep love, and "overstanding" for the struggles, and truth of the black nation."

The black nation is the image of Jah manifested in physical form.

8.Pro-life

Rastafari are Pro Life

Rastafari are "Pro-life." We believe all life is valuable at all times. There are no exceptions to this rule, ever! We value all human life, all plant life, all animal life. We kill nothing, this is why we allow our hair to grow so long and never cut it....because we let! Life! Live! No exceptions!

Because we are pro-life, are also antiwar, anti-fight and anti-argument. Rastafari like peace, with all. Life is of Jah. Rasta promote living life.

9. Love

[20] If anyone says, "I love Jah," and hates his brother, he is a liar; for he who does not love his brother whom he has seen cannot[a] love Jah whom he has not seen. - **1 John 4:19-5:4**

Extensions of Jah Love

As Living extensions of Jah, we as Rasta are in a constant "state" of Love! Love is free...and does not discriminate! With love comes, patience, understanding, respect and a willingness to unite together as one. In all things, Rasta likes to start and finish with "Love."

Love for other Nations

Love for other Nations, as Rasta means that we respect the Culture and beliefs and way of life, of other nations. As Rastafari We do not try to force other nations, nor other people, to believe, what we believe or to live our way of life. There is much to be gained spiritually by appreciating and learning about other cultures, other Nations and other ways of life.

More Love to the Black Nation

Jah Jah made Rasta to send "More Love and understanding" into the black nation. As Rasta we are sensitive to the pain, struggles, needs and opinions of Black men, of Black women and of black children, and we give "more love" to the black nation, as a way to be a solution to problems faced by Africans and not a contributing factor to the pain and struggles.

Love of Self

As Rastafari all Rasta must love themselves without limit and without restriction. This includes your own origin, your facial features, Hair texture, skin-color, eye color etc. Self-Love as Rasta is of the utmost importance. As messengers of love, we know that in order to be effective as Jah messengers we must first love our selves.

Again Rastafari is the answer to the pain and struggles of Black men women and Children who *cried out* during times of biblical slavery. Love is an important part of Rastafari as all types of love are a healing and expression of Jah.

Loving your Brother and Sister
Loving your brother and sister your own nation creates a network of people, a nation strong which can live thrive and survive.

Again, Rastafari was created to heal the black nation and bring us back to our original way of life of as a united thriving, loving and independent nation.

10.Zion

"Zion" is the word Rasta use for "Heaven." Zion is a beautiful and peaceful place where the Sun is always shining and the birds are always chirping. There is no war only love. Jah is there. His Greatness, and his power, radiate and abound!

Zion is on the Minds of the Rastafari people every minute, of every hour, of every day. Zion is where the Most High Roams, and where souls are at rest and at peace. A Rasta prepares his whole life to prepare himself to enter Zion.

He remains humble, does not allow Satan to allow him to stumble on a stumbling block, and avoids Babylon corruption as much as possible.

11. Watch your words

10And he called the multitude, and said unto them, Hear, and understand: **(It is)** Not that which goeth into the mouth defileth a man; but that which cometh out of the mouth, this defileth a man.

Words have Power!

Words have power to heal, and words have power to hurt. Words have power to build up and words have power to destroy.

Think before you speak...Ask yourself...is this something I would say in the presence of the Most High Jah? If the answer is no...you may want to reconsider your words. Jah does judge our words. Because your words come from you heart.

12. Do not watch others!

Watching others is a Babylon favorite pastime, but watching others is upsetting to the Almighty, and a sin under the Rastafari Livity.

Why is watching others a sin under Rastafari?

Watching others creates Satanic opportunities by way of "what is seen."

By giving way to lust, judgment, jealousy envy, greed, perversion etc. Rasta knows we must *turn our heads, or close our eyes* when we see something we are not "invited" to see, that is "unclean or of Babylon.

"Response"-ability of watching others

Sometimes there are things about others it is in our best intrest for us not to know! All knowledge comes with "response" – ability. Which highlights another point...often when we "watch" others and we "see" things we were not meant to see, we will be tempted to "Gossip" which is also a sin, in Jah Jah book.

We are not *qualified* to Judge

When we watch someone uninvited this puts us in a position to be "The Judge." Only the Most High is "The Judge" because he has the authority, wisdom, knowledge, and awareness to be the Judge. We as humans...do not! Don't watch other people, Jah Jah whip you for that!

13. Natural Living

Natural Living is "Zion living." This includes *the food you eat, how you care for your Body, and how you care for and maintain your home/and raise your children.*

Natural Living - Food

I wanted to give an idea of the types of foods Rasta eat on a day to day basis. Here are some foods typical to a Rastafari "Ital" diet.

Seeds and Nuts
Sunflower Seeds
Cashew
Peanuts
Almonds
Peanuts

Dried Fruit
Raisins
Dried Apricots
Dried Cranberries
Dried Ginger

Dried Mango
Dried Pears (my favorite)

Vegetables (earth)
Pumpkin
Dashine
Yam
Potatoes
Squash

Vegtables (other)
Green Banana
Plantain
String beans
Okra
Spinach

Fruits
Bananas
Oranges
Straw Berries
Apples
Plums
Peaches
Mango

Empress Yuajah

Milk;

Almond Milk or Soya Milk Only! <u>Rasta do not believe in drinking Cow's milk.</u> It is nonsensical, and deemed *"unclean."*

Many Rastafari shop at health food Grocery stores, or bulk food stores because we can meet most of our Ital food needs by shopping there.

Natural Living - Home

Home Cleaning

No perfumes (exception for all natural oils)

No Aerosol Spray cans (we know aerosol spray contains harmful chemicals to the environment

"Thursday Plantation" Tea tree Oil

Rasta uses all natural cleaners for cleaning the home and doing chores such as dishes and laundry around the house. I use <u>"Teatree Oil."</u> It's great for cleaning

115

anything in the home including, floors and dishes. It Smells great and it's all natural Just dilute it in some water before using it.

Look for the "Thursday plantation" brand. (Yeah I am not thrilled about the name either) But it really is one of the better brands for "Tea Tree" Oil products.

You can get "Tea Tree" Oil shampoo and deodorant too.

Natural/African Living - Home Living Life

We as Rastafari love to have plants in the home...as they remind us of being outside in the nature like a forest...WE love fish because fish are living and swimming and we love to surround ourselves with the beauties and wonders of "living life" create by Jah. Living life in the home creates the feelings of Jah within the home.

Natural Living - Health

Health and healing
For Health and Healing <u>Rastafari do not believe in taking prescription medications.</u>
We use vitamins, minerals and herbs.

I own a great book for this purpose...it's called...

<u>"The Doctors Complete Guide to Vitamins and Minerals" (Buy it on Amazon.com)</u>

From this book I have learned that there is a vitamin or a mineral you can take for just about anything that ails you. Prescription drugs are not a necessity.

This is a Great book to Guide you to live without the use of Medications!!!

Natural Living - Body Care & Products

Soap;

All natural, without additives or preservatives. Here in Toronto, Canada, we have store called *"Lush."* You can find them online as well. They make all natural soaps and hair care products that smell *out of this world*. My favorite soap is called "Karma."

Toothpaste;

Rasta is aware that there are some potentially harmful ingredients in toothpaste. The most common knowledge of the harm Toothpaste can do to the body is that it can assist in the calcification of the "Pineal Gland," which is one of, our spiritual gateways and psychic (sixth sense) connections.

This may or may not be true. The ingredients on toothpaste are just too long. Rasta use all natural "Neem" toothpaste, or "Tea Tree" toothpaste to brush our teeth. Or you can use plain old baking soda.

Shampoo;

Many people don't give a second thought to the type of shampoo they to wash their hair. As Rastafari we pay special attention to this. Remember our hair is our spiritual Antenna, as Rasta. It is very important that we honour Jah and use Shampoo that is natural, and not harmful to our bodies as our hair is a "sender and receiver" of spiritual energy and, our hair follicles are a super absorbent part of the body.

Many Jamaican Rasta use a mixture of Aloe and lime to wash the Dreadlocks. It is said to help the hair to lock. This works if you go out into the sun immediately after you wash your hair.

Deodorant;
Well, nobody is saying it so I will. Why do you think so many women get breast cancer? I think the answer is 2 fold.

Women need to stop wearing bras with underwire in them.

Women need to stop using deodorant with "Aluminum" listed as its main ingredient.

As Rastafari we use natural deodorant. Check your local health store.

Ital Soup Recipe

You will need....

1 Pound (454) g Yams or about 2 medium sized Yams cut into 2 inch 5 cm pieces

½ pound (227 g) sweet potatoes (1 medium, cut into 2 inch (5 cm) pieces

1 can of coconut milk

3 cups (720 ml) vegetable broth

1 pound (454) fresh pumpkin or butternut squash, peeled and cut into 2 inch (5 cm pieces

½ pound (227 g) carrots (3 medium) peeled and sliced

1 Pound (454g) Fresh callaloo, or 1 can (19 ounces (538 g) callaloo, drained; or ½ pound of spinach and ½ pound (227g) Kale

1 Chayote squash

1 Green pepper

2 medium sized tomatoes

2 cloves garlic

3 spring onions or scallions

5 - 6 cups shredded cabbage

1 hot pepper, minced

Freshly ground black pepper and salt

How to Prepare
<u>Step 1</u>
Place the yams and sweet potatoes in a stockpot with the coconut milk and broth.

Add the pumpkin or squash and carrots.
<u>Step 2</u>

Bring to a boil and simmer for 10 minutes.
<u>Step 3</u>

While the root vegetables simmer, carefully wash the callaloo, trimming away any thick stems. Chop and set asides
<u>Step 4</u>

To peel the chayote squash, cut it lengthwise into quarters and remove the heart. Dice the remaining squash, green pepper, tomatoes, garlic, and spring onions, and add with the shredded cabbage and hot pepper to the stockpot.

Step 5

Simmer for 20 minutes more until the vegetables are tender. Season with plenty of freshly ground black pepper and salt if desired. Puree the vegetables for richer soup. Makes 6 servings

"Run Down" Recipe
Very Popular Jamaican Break Fast

If you want to embrace the Culture of Jamaica, then you have to eat some Run Down at list once on a Saturday Morning with some Fried dumpling. Seriously it hits the spot and may send you back to bed. Lol Don't worry it won't give you a runny stomach. The name comes from the rich gravy of the meal.

You will need...
3 tablespoons of freshly squeezed lime juice

2 lbs. (1 kg) mackerel or other oily fish (salt fish *boneless* works good too)

3 cups (750) coconut milk

1 large onion, diced

2 cloves garlic, sliced

1 scotch bonnet or jalapeno chili, deseeded and minced

1 lb (500 g) ripe tomatoes, blanched, peeled and diced

1 tablespoon cider vinegar

1 tea spoon dried thyme
Salt and freshly ground black pepper (no salt if you are using salt fish)

How to Prepare

Step 1
Pour the lime juice over the fish fillets in a shallow bowl and set aside.

Step 2
IN a large, heavy skillet cook the coconut milk until it turns oily about 5 to 7 minutes.
Step 3
Add the onion, garlic and chili, and cook until tender, about 5 minutes
Stir in the tomatoes, vinegar, thyme, and salt and pepper.
Step 4
Add the fish, cover and cook until the fish flakes easily when tested with a fork, about 10 minutes.

Serves 6 people

Jamaican Curried Tofu Recipe

1 pound of tofu

Light soy sauce

Little bit of salt and freshly ground black pepper

½ teaspoon ground cumin

½ teaspoon garlic powder

½ Teaspoon of Jamaican curry powder

2-3 tablespoons of olive oil

1 medium onion diced

1 medium potato, peeled and cut into cubes

3 / 4 cups of baby carrots

1 medium roma tomato diced

2 scallions chopped

5 sprigs of fresh thyme

½ teaspoon of ground allspice

1 cup of water

1 vegetarian bouillon cube

15 ml of flour

Dissolved in 45 ml of water

Step 1

Drain the Tofu and slice it into 8 - 10 pieces.

Sprinkle both sides lightly with the soy sauce, and season to taste with the salt, black pepper, cumin, garlic powder, and curry powder

Step 2
Heat the oil in a large skillet over medium high heat and add the tofu, and fry on both sides until firm and golden.
Transfer it to a plate and set it aside

Step 3

Add more oil to the skillet if needed, then add the onion, potato, and carrots and saute until tender.

Step 4
Season with a pinch of salt and add the tomato, scallions, thyme, allspice, 1 cup of water and bouillon

Step 5

Bring to a boil, then add the flour and water mixture and cook until the sauce begins to thicken

Step6

Return the tofu to the skillet and simmer for approximately 10 minutes.
serve over rice or vegetables

Makes 6 Servings

14. Dreadlocks

"...All the days of the vow of his separation no <u>razor shall come upon his head;</u> until the days are fulfilled for which he separated himself to the Lord, <u>he shall be holy.</u> Then he shall let the locks of the hair of his head grow..." – **Book of Numbers 6**, *Christian Bible*

Separateness onto Jah

To enter Zion we must separate ourselves from the habits and lifestyle of the Heathen. The Rastafari Dreadlocks is the representation of our promise to live a Jah inspired life. The locks symbolize our "separateness from Babylon unto Jah." Therefor when people say "you don't have to have dreadlocks to be a Rasta," this is not true. It is just a song. That's it! Rastafari is Nazirite vow of Today, only with a new purpose. *You do have to have Dreadlocks to be a TRUE Rasta!*

As a Rastafari, no hair on our entire body should meet a Razor our entire lives. This is just one of the ways that we as Rastafari Honour Jah.

Rasta **not** "Hypnotized" by Babylon

The "Separateness" of Rastafari is real. It is not easy for me living in Babylon surrounded by people who think completely different than me and who are living by different laws than myself, in most cases completely law-less.

Rasta takes "separateness" unto Jah very seriously. We make sure not to allow Bablyon to Hypnotize us with seductions of lust, Vanity, sex, etc.

My Dreadlocks are a reminder of my Covenant with Jah to keep clean and pure, and keep myself far from the ways of Babylon and The Heathen.

Dreadlocks as spiritual "Antenna"

The Rastafari dreadlocks Also serve as an Everlasting physical spiritual Connection (Antennae) to Jah. Adam and Eve, Jah first created humans out of Africa, Also had the same natty dreadlocks. Give thanks and Praises unto the Most High, Jah Rastafari.

Nothing Dreadful about Locks?

I have a woman visiting my blog, insisting she must "school" me on Rastafari. Anyway she said in one of her "rants" on my blog that Rasta does not call Dreadlocks "Dreadlocks" that we call them "Locks" because there is nothing "Dreadful" about having dreadlocks...

Word "Dreadlocks" meaning

This person is missing the point completely about the meaning of the word Dreadlocks. Dreadlocks are called "dread" locks because dread means "to fear." Rasta fear Jah. That is why we keep his Laws and Commandments.

Dreadlocks = "fear of Jah" Locks. Just in case you were wondering, or if you get asked.

15. Honor Jah

As Rastafari Empress and Kingman we honor Jah every day. We do this by...

Listening to Rastafari inspired music

Rasta know that Rasta Reggae Music is the music of Jah. I learned that Reggae music was once known as "Kings Music." This makes perfect sense to my Rastafari heart. Because Kings are high, and "highness" is of Jah.

Wearing our hair in natural dreadlocks

Dreadlocks are a Jah inspired fuss free hairstyle. No combing, no scissors and no styling. African hair worn in dreadlocks is on of the greatest ways to honor Jah of *all.*

Eating clean unprocessed foods

Eating clean unprocessed foods honors Jah because we honor the way he intended for us to eat. Jah did not create McDonalds, Jah did not create Swiss Chalet. Jah gave us, Potatoes, Yam, Apples, Bananas, grapes...All Natural all unprocessed Jah Ital food.

Wearing Rastafari colored Jewelery (Red Yellow and Green)

Rasta Jewelry feels good and it looks beautiful. Jah loves it when we honor him by Saluting Africa and our African Ancestry by wearing African King Selassie I Colors.

Rastafari is a relationship with the Most High. Rasta honor Jah so when we need it...(at the gates of Zion) Jah will honor us.

14. Choose Jah!

We as Rasta know, that everything in life, including all behaviours, all activities, all thoughts...

Fall under only 1 of two categories. *Satan or Jah.* Rasta steers far of things that are of Satan.

A great Rastafari friend of mine told me about a book called *"The Lost Books of The Bible."* He says this book explains that, since the beginning of time, Satan is always trying to recreate everything that Jah creates in order to capture the hearts and minds (and souls) of the people, and turn them away from Jah truth.

Here is a list of some things that are of Satan and some things that are of Jah, to help you Choose Jah...

Some Practices and Habits of Satan
Lustful sex
Lies
Adultery
Witchcraft
Stealing

Prostitution
Suicide
Satan creates these things so that we avoid the commandments and coventant of Jah and follow him instead. The hope is that we will die while living a Satan inspired life and our soul will go straight into hell, where our master awaits our arrival.

Some Habits and practices of Jah

Making love to someone we love and know
Telling the truth instead of lying
Practicing monogamy
Keeping the Tradition and culture of our Ancestors
Loving our own Nation and Appearance.

Jah wants us to live for him and do his work. This way when that time comes we will be clean and blameless in the sight of Jah, and he will welcome us into Zion.

Rasta knows Zion is a place for clean and righteous, Jah fearing people. But, we have to choose Jah to get it.

15. Resist Satan

"All things are lawful for me," but not all things are helpful. All things are lawful for me, but I will not be enslaved by anything." - **1 Corinthians 6:12**

To resist Satan in order that we may enter Zion means to choose Jah. Satan's sins and temptations are many, and often head in a downward spiral. We may choose Satan once, twice, then 3 times... next we are his servants and Satan's way of life, thoughts and deeds become "the norm" or habit for us.

Know when Satan is using you

Many of us try to Rationalize, and "play down" the fact that Satan does indeed have control over us. With Statements like...."she deserved it..." or "I didn't mean it..." or "We were just having fun..."

Be on Guard of Satan At all times

Stand guard and be aware that Satan is in all things, at anytime, anywhere, seeking opportunities to "use" us to work his evil and uncleanliness, and to cause us to sin *Against* the Most High.

Resisting Satans temptations means....
Choosing "high," Royal and clean words when we speak of ourselves and others.

Choosing to replace negative thinking with positive thinking; instead of allowing negative thoughts to repeat them self over and over in our minds.

Staying away from people places and things that tempt us...such as...
Porno,
A gossipy neighbor,
Horror movies,
drugs, etc.

16. No Lust!

Rasta knows Satan is very smart. He has many temptations - Various ways that he captures our minds, then our hearts, then our souls, *including lust.*

What is Lust?

Lust is Satan in the form of sex. Lust ful sex has the power of, Eluding us into thinking the sex we seek or desire is normal and good for us...Next thing we know we may be rearranging our whole lives in order to continue to have this lustful perverted sinful uncontrollable insatiable lustful sex.

Sex should be an experience of sharing love and unity between a man and a woman, who are equal healthy and who love each other.

Lust comes in many forms...

Lust may be considered wanting to have sex with someone because you see the physical differences between them and yourself, and have a "perverted" way of looking at the person.

Definition of "lust"

1. Intense sexual desire or appetite.

2. Uncontrolled or illicit sexual desire or appetite; lecherousness.

3. A passionate or overmastering desire or craving (usually followed by *for*): *a lust for power.*

4. Ardent enthusiasm; zest; relish: *an enviable lust for life.*

The bible on Lust - Romans 1:26

"...**26**For this cause Jah gave them up unto vile affections: for even their women did change the natural use into that which is against nature: **27**And likewise also the men, leaving the natural use of the woman, burned in their lust one toward another; men with men working that which is unseemly, and receiving in themselves that recompense of their error which was meet.

28And even as they did not like to retain Jah in *their* knowledge, Jah gave them over to a reprobate mind, to do those things

which are <u>not convenient;</u> **29**Being filled
with all unrighteousness, fornication,
wickedness, covetousness, maliciousness;
full of envy, murder, debate, deceit,
malignity; whisperers, **30**Backbiters, haters
of Jah, despiteful, proud, boasters,
inventors of evil things, disobedient to
parents, **31**Without understanding,
<u>covenantbreakers,</u> <u>without natural
affection,</u> implacable, unmerciful: **32**Who
knowing the judgment of Jah, that they
which commit such things are worthy of
death, not only do the same, but have
pleasure in them that do them..."

Love & Unity of the spirit
As Rasta, we steer clear of mating with
others who may cause us to feel "out of
control," sexually, or lustful desire. Rasta
believes in unity of the spirit, in love, not
just of the flesh.

9 "Beliefs" of Rasta

"...Jesus said to him, "Have you believed because you have seen me? Blessed are those who have not seen and yet have believed."
John 20:29

Rastafari Principle #1
The Babylon System

The Babylon system is everything that was not created by Jah or does not put Jah intention first, and that breaks down Culture of African Peoples and Traditions.

The Babylon system is the system that all people in every part of the world are forced to live under, including schools, Churches, politics, media, and history books. Babylon is not Jah created way of living, but mans.

The Babylon system is Corruption, destruction, degradation, to unity between nations, and Jah people.

The Babylon system has 5 major Areas ...

The Church system
The School System
The Health care System
The System of Law and Government
The System of Buying and Selling
The School System is the biggest problem in the Babylon System. They say they are preparing people for 'the real world" with brain wash and lies

One of the best things to do is to choose Jah Rastafari. Only through Rastafari did I see myself as a boundless limitless, ever expanding being that can create whatever she wants and be her own person

Only through Rastafari did I see myself as an extension of Jah the Almighty and that my work must help others in some fashion or other.

Only through Rastarfari do I know I have to re-educate my own youth as they are

Educated by Babylon so that they grow up knowing the truth, and not lies.

The Babylon School System

The school System is part of the Babylon system for many reasons.

They lie with the information they give the students /children

They lie "by omission"

Universities and colleges are all about making money

A school should prepare you for life, not just to be a machine that makes money. Many people leave college or university to find out they can't get a job in their field after owing thousands of dollars in school fees.

As for elementary school...what are they really teaching the children anyway?

Elementary School Lied to Me

When I was in Elementary school, I learned that black people were slaves in America. I also learned that natives had

their lands stolen by whites. I had no idea
Africa used to be called Ethiopia. I had no
idea, that native people lived over the
entire continent and due to lies and
brainwash, they had their land stolen from
them. I had no idea that a black woman by
the name of Madam Walker, was the first
self-made black millionaire woman born in
America???

Welcome to Babylon!

The Babylon Health Care System

The health care system is treating people
with pharmaceuticals that they know are
detrimental to health in the long run.

For example; did you know that
antibiotics that are designed to kill
infection also kill the good bacteria in your
body as well? Therefore killing gyour
bodies own defense for warding off illness
in the future?

The Doctors, and pharmacies and
continue to sell these so called
"medicines...and people think taking these
"manmade" concoctions are helping to heal
them and keep them healthy, while they are

really making them more sick in the long run.

Wikipedia on Antibiotic resistance...

"*Genes for resistance to antibiotics, like the antibiotics themselves, are ancient.[4] However, the increasing prevalence of antibiotic-resistant bacterial infections seen in clinical practice stems from antibiotic use both within human medicine and veterinary medicine.*

Any use of antibiotics can increase selective pressure in a population of bacteria to allow the resistant bacteria to thrive and the susceptible bacteria to die off. As resistance towards antibiotics becomes more common, a greater need for alternative treatments arises. However, despite a push for new antibiotic therapies there has been a continued decline in the number of newly approved drugs.[5] Antibiotic resistance therefore poses a significant problem."

The Babylon Church System

The Church system is feeding people with lies, mostly by omission. Not that they intend to do this.

As Rastafari I feel it would be beneficial to everyone if the people in the church system would say that the people the Israelites were black people. Might Change some things, make some interactions more harmonious.

Jesus Christ as a Caucasian

No mention of the people in the bible as black

Pretend black slavery in America did not happen

The System of Law and Government

The system of Law and Government has little to do with African Culture. African peoples are Jah direct decendents as we are made "in his image." The System of Law and Government is Babylon.

Too much Discrimination and profiling against African peoples by police officers

Too many black men in Jail

Not enough black people in positions to create and enforce law

Too much control over the people

The Laws and Government, are not in favor of black people and not really in favor of the general public, but are in favor of the wealthy.

The System of buying and selling

The System of buying and selling is babylon because...it controls people. If you do not work, you do not eat, for the most part, and for most people.

Many people do not like their Jobs (Stress & Misery)

The banks store personal information about how much money we get and how we spend it (No Privacy)

Money means some have and some do not have (Division)

Money is not the root of all evil, but how Babylon controls our actions with money is evil. (Control)

Where is Jah Law?

The Babylon law system is highly corrupt, in so many ways on so many levels. The Trayvon Martin verdict is a prime example. As a Rastafari the question I keep asking myself is, where is Jah law in all of this? What really are they teaching the people, in the schools, in the history books, in the law system...on the TV etc?

Rasta stay out of Babylon Way

Too much corruption, too many lies, too much coercion, too much discrimination...Rasta Know the Babylon system is a sure road to Satan living.

In Babylon, there is not enough love, not enough African teachings, not enough unity etc...Rasta make sure not to become *seduced* by Babylon Culture and to embrace the truth of Life, which is Jah Living – Rastafari! By the way if you want to learn more about the Babylon system, just read the bible, Babylon is mentioned all throughout. Another reason you know Rastafari is the truth.

Rastafari Principle #2
"Judgement"

"...For we must all appear before the judgment seat of Christ, so that each one may receive what is due for what he has done in the body, whether good or evil..." **2 Corinthians 5:10**

Judgement is Vital

You may have heard the Rastafari people mention the word "Judgement." Rasta is born with the light of Jah written on our hearts. The Awareness of Jah Judgement is a very important part of the awareness of Rastafari.

What exactly is "Judgement?"

All people of all Nations must face their own "judgement in front of Jah" When Rasta speak of Judgment, we are speaking of the things that will have to be explained to Jah. Those are acts/deeds that are spiritually "unacceptable" and inexcusable under the laws of the Jah, The Most High.

Empress Yuajah

Complete teaching of Rastafari

I feel it incomplete to write a book about Rastafari beliefs and Overstanding and not to explain things I know bring "Judgement." As an Empress , and a servant of the Most High, it's my responsibility to give you a "complete"teaching.

What deeds brings "Judgement"?

Here is a list of things that bring a clear judgment from the Most High. When that time comes and you meet with him concerning all your deeds during your entire life.

Worship of "other" Gods

Sleeping with someone's wife or husband

A Homosexual Lifestyle

Murder

False Witness

Witchcraft

Jah Judgement is real! He will Judge all you do that breaks his laws. *Both the big and the small, because he is witness to all.*

How to Avoid Jah "Judgement"

If you want to avoid The "Judgement" of Jah, it's very simple

Respect all living life
Respect all marriage
Have straight sex or remain celibate
Do not bear false witness
If you are a prostitute stop doing it
Don't Steal
Don't have anything to do with the Occult
Worship only Jah
Keep the 10 commandments

If something of someone causes you to sin, stay away from it or get rid of it.

Never too late to start a new

If you have committed sinful acts in the past, it is never too late to ask for forgiveness from Jah and then eliminate the behavior from your life, and start anew. Jah is merciful but only to those who ask for his forgiveness and recognize their wrong, and eliminate the sinful/unrighteous behaviors and patterns from their life.

"...And if anyone's name was not found written in the book of life, he was thrown into the lake of fire..." - **_Revelation 20:15_**

Rastafari Principle #3
"More Love"

Rasta believes that "More Love" given to many disagreements can solve many problems.

From love comes understanding, forgiveness, unity (togetherness) patience, trust, vulnerability, Kindness...When we give more love we both come out on top.

I have personally put this Rastafari belief into practice many times in my life...only to find that...it works! People want to know they can trust you, that you are not out to hurt them, that they can be vulnerable with you. You can turn many enemies into friends with "More Love." I have done it.

How to give "more love" to another

*Speak from your heart, instead of from
your mind*

*Be Gentle with the feelings of others, by
choosing your words wisely/kindly*

*Try to see things from the other person's
perspective, instead of just your own*

*Come in peace, not in opposition, or an "I
must win" mind set*

Listen to the words the person is saying

*Make an internal vow to forgive those who
have hurt you knowingly or unknowingly*

*Start anew. Make a commitment to live
from today, leave the past behind.*

Rastafari Principle #4
Karma

Rastafari believe strongly in Karma, but it is not something we think about too deeply because we know our actions bring about <u>good</u> Karma. We as Rasta believe that karma is something that you experience according to the energy you send out to other people via your thoughts, intentions and actions.

We As Rastafari believe that our words, deeds and thoughts <u>always come back to us</u>. Sometimes instantaneously sometimes later on. Rasta does believe in Karma, that is why we always try to put out "good vibes."

When speaking with people we use uplifting and positive words
Try to make your actions and motivations pleasing to The Most High

Choose to think good thoughts so that good will come back to us. Jah Rastafari.

Rastafari Principle #5
Choose your friends wisely

Rastafari believe we have to watch who our friends are, very carefully because these are the people who we will become more alike in the future.

People rub off on each other
It is a fact the people you spend time with "rub off" on you and you on them. Examine your current friendships... are these people you would like to emulate? You will... if you are not already doing so.

Like "Capleton," Rastafari Reggae music artist says "...choose your friends and choose them wisely..."

"Friends" hinder entrance to Zion
It is important to choose our Friends wisely as Rasta. Because Zion is our desire and our destiny and we want to avoid any possible hindrances.

Through our friends we may become, jealous, angry, lustful etc...in our hearts and minds. We may commit acts such as Witchcraft, adultery, theft, slander etc. The people whom we spend time with we become more like. This is a belief deeply rooted in the Mind of Rastafari.

Rastafari Principle #6.
"Non- Attachment"

This is a very important "belief" of Rastafari. Rasta knows Babylon designs fancy cars, and expensive clothes, and big houses, etc to distract us from the truth, which is Jah and Holy living.

Rasta does not believe in a materialistic, greed driven lifestyle, nor in the accumulation of "stuff." We know that our sense of self-worth <u>does not come from what we own</u>, or how we dress, or from our physical appearance, but that our sense of self-worth really comes from our hearts and our love of Jah. Because from Jah we get all things, and through Jah all is possible unlimited and infinite.

Bob Marley also believed in Non-Attachment. I just love this youbute video where he explains to the interviewer that he is giving away his Millions.

Rastafari Principle #7
Self-Control and Humbleness

As Rastafari we believe every individual must be responsible for his or her own actions. King Selassie I did not become a King by being irresponsible and building a negative reputation for himself. If you want to be a king you will need a clean past, and a good reputation. If you want to see the Kingdom of Jah , you will have to

avoid slackness and

Have control over your words and your reactions to people and situations

You will have to humble yourself

And practice patience and understanding even when it may seem difficult to do so.

How to build Humbleness

We read our bible every morning and every night

Arguments we do not eavesdrop on them, nor do things that perpetuate arguments

Satanic Music, we avoid music with swearing and references of disrespect of women or men or a people

We avoid watching "Cops and Robbers" shows as Rasta knows these things are Babylon poison for the mind. Before you know it, you will be emulating the words, and mental attitudes, of these sounds, images, and people, if we are not careful

Rastafari Principle # 8
Charity

"...Whoever oppresses a poor man insults his Maker, but he who is generous to the needy honors him..." **Proverbs 14:31** .

Rastafari believe that those who have a lot of money have been given a "blessing" and a Responsibility by the Most High.

Hoarding Money is a Sin!
Rastafari believe that for one to know there are poor people who could make great use of the money that we are "saving" and yet continue to hoard, as numbers on a bank statement...is a sin. Jah does not like this!

As Rastafari we "know" that to have a lot of money means we are chosen to act as "Delivers" and "caregivers" to/of the poor and needy and that the "responsibility" iso <u>share</u> the money that we have been blessed with.

Wealth and Abundance a duty

1. We were chosen by Jah to have this great wealth
2. It is our duty as Servants of Jah to Share the wealth with the poor and the needy

To have food to eat each day is a "Blessing." As Rasta, we are very aware that every time we fill our bellies with food, there is someone that is going without food.

Rastafari believe in Charity to the poor, needy, and the hungry as this is a way to live as servants of Jah and use money as an instrument to help others instead of hoarding money for our own egos.

How I support Charity as Rasta

I usually take myself out for something nice to eat each time I get paid. I also will buy a homeless person on the street something to eat or drink, big or small. I acknowledge them with a smile, and entertain them with some conversation. I know Jah is watching and doing this creates good Karma for me.

Charity big and small

You could buy someone a $5 or $10 meal, once, a week or once every 2 weeks. Your belly is full, so why not help someone else's belly to be full too! Rastafari.

Rastafari Principle # 9
Equal Rights and Justice

"...Learn to do good; seek justice, correct oppression; bring justice to the fatherless, plead the widow's cause..." - **_Isaiah 1:17_**

Equal Rights for all, always!
Everybody deserves Equal Rights and equal treatment, Regardless of Age, socio-economic status, Culture, Religious Beliefs, or Skin Color/ or Ethnicity.

Rasta are born to Stand up for Injustice
In other words, to be a witness to something "unjust" as Rasta, means it is an opportunity *to direct and create change.* Rasta support righteousness and Equal Rights, big and small for all, at any and all times. Jah Jah is watching, we want to make him proud.

I have exercised this principle in my life many times. If I over hear someone disrespecting another....I will stand up.

Nyahbinghi Order Guidelines

I thought it a good idea to insert the Nyabinghi order guidelines into the "Beliefs" Section.

What is Nyahbinghi?

"...During the earlier years of European occupation of Africa, Nyahbinghi was a revolutionary order devoted to preserving the spiritual and cultural integrity of the ancient African way of life. Nyahbinghi brothers and sisters were noted for their royal appearance, proud demeanour..."

"...The Nyahbinghi congregation of faithfuls is the cornerstone of the Rastafari faith, upholding the Bahtawi/Nazarene covenant and the integrity of everliving life..."

Guidelines for Men

The Nyahbinghi Man must abide by the laws of His Imperial Majesty.

It is also the sole duty of every Nyahbinghi Man to uphold the livity of Emperor Haile Selassie I. Thus, every Nyahbinghi Man must see to it that love and harmony be maintained at every Nyahbinghi gathering including House Reasoning.

During I-semble, the Nyahbinghi man is permitted to administrate around the altar or to prophecy before the congregation on His Imperial Majesty Emperor Haile Selassie I, black history and other aspects of Rastafari Ivine livety.

Nyahbinghi man must be skilled on the drums. He should be attired in modest and proper apparel and must uncover his head during an I-semble.

The Binghi man is expected to give his strength towards administering the Theocratic Government of Emperor Haile Selassie I. He may contribute in the governmental admininstration whereever he is capable of giving strength as seen fit by the House. He should also strive to improve his livity and skills/education so that he may be of greater strength to the administration of the Theocracy of Emperor Haile Selassie I.

He should abide with one queen as perfect example set by His Imperial Majesty, Emperor Haile Selassie I. He must be loyal to his queen at all times. If there is a misunderstanding between him and his queen, the matter should be brought before the Priest or the Council of Elders who will deal with the matter privately and constructively.

It is the duty of every Nyahbinghi Man to properly maintain his children and raise them in the order of righteousness. It is wrong for a Nyahbinghi man to trim and comb his children. This is an abomination. The Nyahbinghi man must abstain from whoredom, adultery, fornication and all sinful acts that are an abomination to the Most High. He should keep his temple clean, refraining from use of flesh, drugs, alcohol and all harmful articles of food that are forbidden. The Nyahbinghi man is nonviolent, non-abusive and non- partisan. He must also be free from all criminal or corrupted activities as a true son of JAH Rastafari.

Guidelines for Women (Daughters)

The Nyahbinghi woman must abide by Emperor Haile Selassie I Ivine laws. During I-semble, the Nyahbinghi women are responsible for the teaching of the children with special emphasis on the Amharic languages, His Imperial Majesty Emperor Haile Selassie I, Black History and other aspects of Rastafari Ivine livety.

She is not permitted to administrate around the altar or to prophecy before the congregation. A Nyahbinghi queen does not play the drums at an I-semble but does play the SHAKA (Shaker) or TIMBREL. She may participate in governmental administration, as in the taking of minutes, writing/reading of letters or any other works she is capable of doing, as seen by the House. She should also strive to improve her livity and skills/education so that she may be of greater strength to the Theocracy of Emperor Haile Selassie I and the family.

She must be attired in modest apparel at all times and must not wear pants or revealing garments. Her head must be covered during an I-semble or when congregating among the brethren or outside her gates.

As H.I.M. is the Head of the Nyahbinghi Order, the Nyahbinghi queen must recognise her kingman as her head. She must be loyal to her king head in all things concerning righteousness and at all times. If there is a misunderstanding between her

and her king man, the matter should be
brought before the priest or the Council of
Elders who will deal with the matter
privately and constructively.
During her monthly issue (period of 7
days), the Nyahbinghi queen does not
attend, I-semble or congregate among the
brethrens.

When the Nyahbinghi queen brings forth a
prince, she should stay away from an I-
semble for a period of 3 months. If she
brings forth a princess, she should stay
away for a period of 4 months.

The Nyahbinghi woman must abstain from
whoredom, adultery, fornication and all
sinful acts that are an abomination to the
Most High. She should keep her temple
clean, refraining from use of flesh, drugs,
alcohol and all harmful articles of food that
are forbidden. The wearing of jewelry is not
forbidden but the piercing of the ears is
against the will of JAH. The plaiting of locks
is forbidden as it is written in the book of II
Peter 3: 3, "Whose adorning let it not be

that outward adorning of plaiting the hair."
The Nyahbinghi woman is nonviolent, non-
abusive and non- partisan. She must also be
free from all corruption as a true daughter
of JAH Rastafari.

Bob Marley

"...You can fool some people sometimes,
but you can't fool all the people all the
time..."
-   "Get up Stand-up"

Bob Marley is a Rastafari Hero

Bob Marley was a Rastafari but he is also considered one of Rastafari is "great heroes" because of his notoriety and his success in bringing "Kings music" Reggae music, to the masses.

Bob Marley Music Reflects Rasta Principles

Again Rastafari is a faith/ way of life of Jah, implemented by him...for the purpose of...

Guiding black people out of slavery into independence, and into healing

Teach black people how to live as Independent Africans Again...

Teach the black nation how to live peaceably with other nations

Teach the black nation how to "live clean" in order to enter Zion

Bob Marleys songs show parallels between the *Principles of Rastafari* and the lyrics of his Rastafari song lyrics.

Bob Marley Song Titles

"Get up stand up" (equal rights and justice)
"Africa Unite" (unity)
"One Love" (the belief of more love)
"No more war" (pro-life)
"Forever Loving Jah" (honur Jah)
"Rat Race" (freedom of self)
"Zion Train" (living for zion)
"The black survivors" (Self Reliance)

The list goes on and on....

I have included some song titles and lyrics of Bob Marleys Music, so that we can see in his lyrics *The Rastafari Principles and Beliefs* in his music.

"Rat Race"
Uh! Ya too rude!
Uh! Eh! OH What a rat race!
Oh, what a rat race!
Oh, what a rat race!

Oh, what a rat race!
This is the rat race! Rat race! (Rat race!)
Some a lawful, some a bastard, some a
jacket:
Oh, what a rat race, yeah! Rat race!
Some a gorgon-a, some a hooligan-a, some a
guine-gog-a
In this 'ere rat race, yeah!
Rat race!
I'm singin' that
When the cat's away,
The mice will play.
Political violence fill ya city, ye-ah!
Don't involve Rasta in your say say;
Rasta don't work for no C.I.A.
Rat race, rat race, rat race! Rat race, I'm
sayin':
When you think is peace and safety:
A sudden destruction.
Collective security for surety, ye-ah!
<u>Don't forget your history;</u>
<u>Know your destiny:</u>
In the abundance of water,
The fool is thirsty.
Rat race, rat race, rat race!
Rat race!

Oh, it's a disgrace
To see the human-race
In a rat race, rat race!
You got the horse race;
You got the dog race;
You got the human-race;
But this is a rat race, rat race! (freedom of
self)

"Forever Loving Jah"

Wo-o-o-o! Ya-ya-ya-ya-ya-ya-ya! Woy-
oh!
Yeah-yeah-yeah, yeah-yeah, yeah-yeah-
yeah-yeah! Oh!
(We'll be forever loving Jah;
We'll be forever loving Jah!)
Some they say see them walking up the
street;
They say we're going wrong to all the
people we meet;
But-a we won't worry, we won't shed no
tears:
We found a way to cast away the fears,
Forever, yeah!
(We'll be forever loving Jah) We'll be

forever!

(We'll be forever loving Jah) Forever, yes, and forever!

(We'll be forever loving Jah) There'll be no end.

So, old man river, don't cry for me;

A-have got a running stream of love you see.

So, no matter what stages - oh stages -

Stages - stages they put us through,

We'll never be blue

No matter what rages, oh rages,

Changes - rages they put us through,

We'll never be blue:

We'll be forever, yeah!

(We'll be forever loving Jah) We'll be forever!

(We'll be forever loving Jah) Forever, and ever, yes, and forever!

(We'll be forever loving Jah) 'Cause there is no end.

'Cause only a fool lean upon -

Lean upon his own misunderstanding, oh ho, oh, yeah!

And then what has been hidden

From the wise and the prudent

Been revealed to the babe and the suckling
In everyt'ing, in every way, I say, yeah!
(We'll be forever loving Jah) We'll be
forever!
(We'll be forever loving Jah)
'Cause just like a tree planted - planted by
the rivers of water
That bringeth forth fruits - bringeth forth
fruits in due season;
Everything in life got its purpose,
Find its reason in every season,
Forever, yeah!
(We'll be forever loving Jah) We'll be
forever!
(We'll be forever loving Jah) On and on and
on!
(We'll be forever loving Jah) We'll be
forever, yes, yes -
we'll be forever.
(We'll be forever loving Jah)

"The Black Survivors"
(Ow, ow-ow-ow-ow!
Ow, ow-ow-ow-ow!)
Yeah, yeah, yeah!
How can you be sitting there

Telling me that you care -
That you care?
When every time I look around,
The people suffer in the suffering
In every way, in everywhere. (this refers to
babylon living)
Say: na-na-na-na-na (na-na, na-na!):
We're the survivors, yes: the Black
survivors!
I tell you what: some people got everything;
Some people got nothing;
Some people got hopes and dreams;
Some people got ways and means.
Na-na-na-na-na (na-na, na-na!):
We're the survivors, yes: the Black
survivors!
Yes, we're the survivors, like Daniel out of
the lions' den
(Black survivors) Survivors, survivors!
So I Idren, I sistren,
A-which way will we choose?
We better hurry; oh, hurry; oh, hurry; wo,
now!
'Cause we got no time to lose.
Some people got facts and claims;
Some people got pride and shame;

Some people got the plots and schemes;
Some people got no aim it seems!
Na-na-na-na-na, na-na, na!
We're the survivors, yes: the Black
survivors!
Tell you what: we're the survivors, yeah! -
the Black survivors, yeah!
We're the survivors, like Shadrach,
Meshach and Abednego
(Black survivors),
Thrown in the fire, but-a never get burn.
So I Idren, I-sistren,
The preaching and talkin' is done;
We've gotta live up, wo now, wo now! -
'Cause the Father's time has come.
Some people put the best outside;
Some people keep the best inside;
Some people can't stand up strong;
Some people won't wait for long.
(Na-na-na-na-na!) Na-na-na, na-na-na na!
We're the survivors
In this age of technological inhumanity
(Black survival),
Scientific atrocity (survivors),
Atomic misphilosophy (Black survival),
Nuclear misenergy (survivors):

It's a world that forces lifelong insecurity
(Black survival).
Together now:
(Na-na-na-na-na!) Na na-na na na! (Na na-
na na na!)
We're the survivors, yeah!
We're the survivors!
Yes, the Black survivors!
We're the survivors:
A good man is never honoured
   *(This is applicable to the Life and story of
Marcus Garvey - Jah Prophet)*
   (survivors)
in his own country (Black survival).
Nothing change, nothing strange
(survivors).
Nothing change, nothing strange (Black
survivors).
We got to survive, y'all! (survivors) -
[fadeout]

Zion Train

Zion train is coming our way;
The Zion train is coming our way;
Oh, people, get on board! (you better get on

board!)
Thank the Lord (praise Fari) -
I gotta catch a train, 'cause there is no other
station;
Then you going in the same direction (ooh-
ooh).
Zion's train is coming our way;
The Zion's train is coming our way.
<u>Which man can save his brother's soul?</u>
(save your brother's soul)
Oh man, it's just <u>self-control.</u> (oo-hoo-oo!)
Don't gain the world and lose your soul
(just don't lose your soul)
Wisdom is better than silver and gold -
To the bridge (ooh-ooh!)
Oh, where there's a will,
There's always a way.
Where there's a will,
There's always a way (way, way, way, way),
Soul train is coming our way; er!
Zion train is coming our way.
Two thousand years of history (history)
Could not be wiped away so easily.
Two thousand years of history (Black
history)
Could not be wiped so easily (could not be

wiped so easily).
Oh, children, Zion train is comin' our way;
get on board now!
They said the Zion train is comin' our way;
you got a ticket, so thank the Lord!
Zion's train is - Zion's train is - Zion's train
is - Zion's train -
They said the soul train is coming our way;
They said the soul train is coming our way.

Slave Driver
Ooh-ooh-oo-ooh. Oo-oo-ooh! Oo-oo-ooh.
Slave driver, the table is turn; (catch a fire)
Catch a fire, so you can get burn, now.
(catch a fire)
Slave driver, the table is turn; (catch a fire)
Catch a fire: gonna get burn. (catch a fire)
Wo, now!
Ev'rytime I hear the crack of a whip,
My blood runs cold.
I remember on the slave ship,
How they brutalize the very souls.
Today they say that we are free,
Only to be chained in poverty.
Good God, I think it's illiteracy;
It's only a machine that makes money.

Slave driver, the table is turn, y'all. Ooh-
ooh-oo-ooh.
Slave driver, uh! The table is turn, baby,
now; (catch a fire)
Catch a fire, so you can get burn, baby, now.
(catch a fire)
Slave driver, the table is turn, y'all; (catch a
fire)
Catch a fire: so you can get burn, now.
(catch a fire)
Ev'rytime I hear the crack of a whip,
My blood runs cold.
I remember on the slave ship,
How they brutalize the very soul.
O God, have mercy on our souls!
Oh, slave driver, the table is turn, y'all;
(catch a fire)
Catch a fire, so you can get burn. (catch a
fire)
Slave driver, the table is turn, y'all; (catch a
fire)
Catch a fire ... /fadeout/

King Selassie I

You may be wondering...how did King Selassie I become a part of Jah plan?
Why is King Selassie I so special in Rastafari?

Under the Section "what Jah <u>is</u>" I explained the following...
Jah is the Almighty Creator
Jah is an African Entity
Jah is loving and merciful
Jah is listening and faithful
Jah sees and knows all things

What does Jah Want?

Ansering the question what does Jah want, will help you to understand how and why Rastafari came into existence. It will also help me create a outline for explaining the spirituality of Rastafari.

Many people wonder....what does Jah want? The answer is very simple...

Jah wants to be glorified forever and ever Amen. Jah wants people to know he is in fact real. Jah wan

Jah wants people to stop calling out names of Gods that do not exist

Jah wants people to stop bowing down to idols, hand crafted that have no significance

Jah wants people to stop giving into the temptations and lifestyle of Satan

Jah wants the direct decedents of his first people, to be loved appreciated and honored

Jah wants his direct descendants to love appreciate and honor themselves.

Jah wants people to live clean so that he can set a place for them in Zion

Jah is real and he created Rasta since conception, with the single purpose to glorify his name, and bring people to his light.

Jah created the life of King Selassie I for a very specific purpose...

To protect the land where the first man and woman were created
To glorify his own name (Jah)
To demonstrate the lineage of Christ
To fulfill the promise sit upon the throne of King David.
Before I go any further I should explain that
Rastafari has many levels, so to speak.
We are not a Religion so to speak, but we deserve to get the same Respect and apprection that Religion gets, considering Rastafari is the only real faith on the planet.

I will discuss this a little more later.
There is much I would like to explain about
The link between Jah and King Selassie I
The link between Rasta and Jah
The Link between Rasta and King Selassie I

For you to get a full understanding of Rastafari

King Selassie I protected The Garden of Eden

Jah is the Almighty, he sees and knows the hearts of all man. Before Musilini invaded Ethiopia, Jah knew exactly who and when this would take place. Jah created from birth King Selassie I, to protect the land of the Garden of Eden

Rasta Glorify the Name of King Selassie forever

Ultimately, Iyasu was deposed on the grounds of conversion to another Religion. King Selassie is the Same Linage as Christ.

King Selassie I Reign is the promise of Jah to King David fulfilled

King Selassie I

"...We must stop confusing religion and spirituality...Due to human imperfection religion has become corrupt, political, and divisive..." – **King Selassie I Emperor of Ethiopia 1930 – 1974**

Revelation 5
The seven-sealed Book

*"And I saw in the right hand of Him that sat
on the throne a BOOK written within and on
the backside, SEALED with SEVEN SEALS.
And I saw a strong angel proclaiming with a
loud voice, WHO is worthy to OPEN the
BOOK, and to LOOSE the SEALS thereof?
And NO MAN in heaven, nor in earth, neither
under the earth, was able to open the book,
neither to look thereon. And I wept much,
because no man was found worthy to open
and to read the BOOK, neither to look
thereon."*

*"And one of the elders saith unto me, Weep
not: behold, the LION of the tribe of Juda, the
Root of David, hath prevailed to OPEN the
BOOK, and to LOOSE the SEVEN SEALS
thereof. And I beheld, and, lo, in the midst of
the throne and of the four beasts, and in the
midst of the elders, stood a LAMB as it had
been slain, having seven horns and seven
eyes, which are the SEVEN Spirits of GOD
sent forth into all the earth. And HE came*

and TOOK the BOOK out of the right hand of Him that sat upon the throne.

When I saw a photo of King Selassie I for the first time...

Something went "on" like a light bulb in my mind. "This man has something to do with my spirituality" I thoughts. By about the 4th and 5th photo of the King that I was shown, I said to myself..."this man is my spirituality!"

A Rastafari heart is full of "knowing" that others may not be able to make sense of. But many know that a Rastafari "knowing" is Real.

I have put together some information to help you Overstand the Divinity of King Selassie I.

King Selassie I and the 7 Seals

"...And I saw a strong angel proclaiming with a loud voice, WHO is worthy to OPEN

the BOOK, and to LOOSE the SEALS thereof? And NO MAN in Heaven, nor in earth, neither under the earth, was able to open the book, neither to look thereon. And I wept much, because no man was found worthy to open and to read the BOOK, neither to look thereon." - ***Revelation 5:5***
   "Lion tribe of Judah"

"And one of the elders saith unto me, Weep not: behold, *the LION of the tribe of Judah, the Root of David, hath prevailed to OPEN the BOOK, and to LOOSE the SEVEN SEALS thereof.* And I beheld, and, lo, in the midst of the throne and of the four beasts, and in the midst of the elders, stood a LAMB as it had been slain, having seven horns and seven eyes, which are the SEVEN Spirits of GOD sent forth into all the earth. And HE came and TOOK the BOOK out of the right hand of Him that sat upon the throne."

King Selassie I Crowing title

Haile Selassie's full title in office is "His Imperial Majesty Haile Selassie I, Conquering Lion of the Tribe of Judah, King of Kings of Ethiopia, Elect of God".[nb 3]

Same Lineage of King David

His Crowing title reflects Ethiopian dynastic traditions, which hold that all monarchs must trace their lineage back to Menelik I, who in the Ethiopian tradition was the offspring of King Solomon and the Queen of Sheba.[20]

225th decedent to sit on throne of King David- Jeremiah 33:10

"...For thus saith the LORD; David shall never want a man to sit upon the throne of the house of Israel..."

The Meaning of the Name Haile Selassie I

Haile Selassie translates to "Power of the Trinity".

The "Tribe of Judah"
(The tribe of Emperor Haile Selassie I)
Haile Selassie I is "the conquering Lion of **the Tribe of Judah.**" I wanted to outline the Tribe of Judah in the bible, so you could really "Overstand" the Divine Royal Lineage of Emperor Haile Selassie I.

"12 Tribes of Israel" Split
"After the reign of King Solomon, around 980 BC, the kingdom of Israel split. The ten northern tribes rebelled against King Rehoboam, the son of Solomon, the son of David, of the tribe of Judah. It should be noted that one of the ten tribes that rebelled, Simeon, was actually south of Judah and Benjamin, but more distant from Jerusalem. Judah, along with Benjamin, was the two southern tribes that remained loyal to Rehoboam, who reigned from the capital city of Jerusalem. Like Judah, the lands of Benjamin were near Jerusalem. The ten northern tribes (including Simeon) made Jeroboam, (a son of one of Solomon's servants,) their king instead of Rehoboam.

The split of the kingdom of Israel occurred when the new King Rehoboam told Israel that he would make their burdens heavier, rather than lighter, than his father Solomon had done.

Rehoboam told Israel in 1 Kings 12:14, "... *My father made your yoke heavy, and I will add to your yoke: my father also chastised you with whips, but I will chastise you with scorpions.*"

These words provoked rebellion by the northern tribes, but 1 Kings 12:15 tells us that "... *the cause was from the LORD, that he might perform his saying, which the LORD spake by Ahijah the Shilonite unto Jeroboam* ...." This was as prophesied near the end of Solomon's reign, in 1 Kings 11:31, when the prophet Ahijah said to Jeroboam, "... *thus saith the LORD, the God of Israel, Behold, I will rend the kingdom out of the hand of Solomon, and will give ten tribes to thee* (Jeroboam) ...." In 1 Kings 11:33 the prophet gives God's reason, "*Because that they have forsaken me, and have worshipped Ashtoreth the goddess of the Zidonians, Chemosh the god of the Moabites, and Milcom the god of the children of Ammon, and have not walked in my ways, to do that which is right in mine eyes, and to keep my statutes and my judgments, as did David his* (Solomon's) *father."*

Then in 1 Kings 11:34-35 we see that the split would actually occur during Rehoboam's reign, not during Solomon's lifetime.

"Howbeit I will not take the whole kingdom out of his hand: but I will make him (Solomon) *prince all the days of his life for David my servant's sake, whom I chose, because he kept my commandments and my statutes: But I will take the kingdom out of his son's hand* (Rehoboam's hand)*, and will give it unto thee* (Jeroboam)*, even ten tribes."*

So the ten tribes were not removed from the royal line of David and Solomon until after Solomon had died.

Once the split occurred, it was maintained and deepened by the wicked actions of Jeroboam in 1 Kings 12:26-31, who set up false gods to be worshipped by the northern tribes.

"... Jeroboam said in his heart, Now shall the kingdom return to the house of David: If this people go up to do sacrifice in the house of the LORD at Jerusalem, then shall the heart of this people turn again unto their lord, even unto Rehoboam king of Judah, and they shall kill me, and go again to Rehoboam king of Judah. Whereupon the king took counsel, and made two calves of gold, and said unto them, It is too much for you to go up to Jerusalem: behold thy gods, O Israel, which brought thee up out of the land of Egypt. And he set the one in Bethel, and the other put he in Dan. And this thing became a sin: for the people went to worship before the one, even unto Dan. And he made an house of high places, and made priests of the lowest of the people, which were not of the sons of Levi."

The 10 Northern tribes of Israel

The term "Israel" usually refers to the entire nation, all of the tribes, but sometimes in the old testament, it refers just to the northern kingdom of *ten tribes* (of Israel), as is the case in the passage above. The ten are Reuben, Simeon, Dan, Naphtali, Gad, Asher, Issachar, Zebulun, Ephraim, and Manasseh.

The two Southern Tribes of Israel

The southern tribes were Judah and Benjamin. **<u>Since Judah was the larger tribe, and the line of kings came through them,</u>** the southern kingdom became known as the kingdom of Judah. Since the temple was in Jerusalem in the south, much of the priestly tribe of Levi remained in the south. It should be noted that since Ephraim was the largest of the tribes in the north, God sometimes refers to the northern kingdom as "Ephraim". The two split kingdoms never reunited..."

King Selassie I is of "The Conquering Lion
of The tribe of Judah..._

Protected the Garden of Eden

The Second Italo–Ethiopian War, also referred to as the Second Italo–Abyssinian War, was a colonial war that started in October 1935 and ended in May 1936. The war was fought between the armed forces of the Kingdom of Italy (Regno d'Italia) and the armed forces of the Ethiopian Empire (also known at the time as Abyssinia). The war resulted in the military occupation of Ethiopia.

– *Wikipedia.com*

In 1935 Mussolini and his troops invaded Ethiopia with the intention to colonize the land. many people do not know that the entire Continent of Africa used to be called "Ethiopia" and that due to the process of continued Colonization for foreign invaders, "Ethiopia" is now known as "Africa"

Back to King Selassie I. The specific spot that was yet to be colorized is where Jah placed the first man and the first woman – (Adam and Eve) in The Garden of Eden. But Jah Jah was prepared! King Selassie I was there, and he was not going to have any colonization of his land. King Selassie I only had a small Army. He eventually sought the help of Queen Elizabeth, and The Brittish Army and was able to defeat Mussolini and his Italian Army. This is why Ethiopia still has its *original name* today. Give thanks and praise unto the Most High Jah Rastafari! Jah works is magnificent!

King Selassie's Speech - "Spirituality"

"The temple of "The Most high" begins with the human body, which houses our life, essence of our existence. Africans are in bondage today because they approach spirituality through Religion provided by foreign invaders and conquerors. We must stop confusing religion and spirituality. Religion is a set of rules, regulations and rituals created by humans which were supposed to help people grow spiritually."

"Due to human imperfection religion has become corrupt, political, and divisive and a tool for power struggle. Spirituality is not theology or ideology. It is simply a way of life, pure and original as was given by "The Most high". Spirituality is a network linking us to "The Most high", the universe and each other. As the essence of our existence it embodies our culture, true identity, nationhood and destiny. A people without a nation they can really call their own is a people without a soul. Africa is our nation and is in spiritual and physical bondage because her leaders are turning to outside forces for solutions to African problems when everything Africa needs is within her. When African righteous people come together, the world will come together. This is our divine destiny."

1. "Africans are in bondage because they approach spirituality through Religion..."
2. "We must stop confusing Religion with Spirituality...Religion is a set of rules, regulations and rituals created by humans..."
3. "Due to human imperfection Religion has become corrupt..."

4. "Spirituality is a "way of life" ...of which embodies our culture, true identity, nationhood and destiny..."

5. "Everything Africa needs is within her..." (all the needs of black people can be met within the black community)

6. The world is out of spiritual balance because "When African righteous people come together, the world will come together."

"Peace No More War" - Speech

I just found this speech the same day I was publishing the book. It touched my heart. Also I should tell you as Rastafari we give just as much respect and honor to Empress Menen Because *the King and Queen were crowned the same time.*
Empress Menen is known as The "Queen of Queens."
Here is the speech I found.

"I am pleased to present my speech to all world women.
When Italy conquered our people and country the world women Association supported us to settle peace and freedom. We are very happy to express our deep feeling for the association.
When I am speaking now in order to be understood to all countries my daughter princess Tsehaye translated my speech into English language.
Princess Tsehaye made speech as follows. During this time Italy conquered us

difficulty unjustly and world women should hear their voice.

Even though world women are living in different countries with different climate, all women are interrelated with the same will and objectives.

War is distress and trouble of mankind, all world women are in different countries, different race, religion the act of violence and war victimized their husbands, brothers and children. War is a destruction of the family and can make people immigrant. So women are against war. We know that all Italian mothers and barren women may worry about the war, since war is good for nothing. Therefore, all women found in the world should prevent the war before it brings trouble and distress. They should collaborate their voice and request to avoid the war before the bloodshed comes on both sides. Ethiopia do not think to act the violence conflict, here wish is to maintain peace. Ethiopia tried to settle the conflict peacefully in early months. In every aspect Ethiopia has done her best. So we are mentally free.

Ethiopian people welcomed any foreigners, guests who came to work peacefully and innocently, Ethiopian people good hospitality to foreigners has been narrated in the history of the world. However, one state is which is neighbor to Ethiopia is trying to control and govern. Ethiopia is always on the line of peace, while the rival state is looking only its own interest.

The enemy deployed its army and based around our country to kill our women's husbands, children, and brothers. Our people live working peacefully being God fearing but the enemy is trying to devastate the wealth of the country and destroy our family in the name of modernization.

We pray to God not to face such kind of distress and destruction if the so called modernization brings a big trouble.

Hence, the association which is established for the purpose of peace by world women may exert influence to bring peace and stability. We don't hesitate that world women Association may contribute a lot to settle this conflict peacefully.

We pray to god that the Association to accomplish its mission. We hope the act of the Association may bring fruitful result to preserve peace and security in our country. Nonetheless, if the war is started, we women should treat wounded soldiers and minimize the trouble of the war.
Women who are living all over the world who stand for peace may help us during the war time. We know that these women assist the sacrificed patriot's family.
All women of the world should struggle to bring peace and justice. Government officials may guided on the line of God, we pray for this and you may collaborate with us."

How to Enter Zion

"...For many are called, but few are chosen..." - **_Matthew 22:14_**

What is Zion Like?

Zion is a place where the weather is always nice. The birds are always chirping, the trees, grass and bushes are all manicured and maintained, and the Sun is always shining, Zion is also known as heaven. In Zion there is no crime, no poverty, and no negative energy to speak of. Zion is full of love, full of harmony, and all souls who are in Zion are at peace and at rest.

The Christian Bible on How to get into Zion. Peter 2

3 - "His divine power has given us everything we need for life and Godliness through our knowledge of him who called us by his own glory and goodness. Through these he has given us his very great and precious promises, so that through them you may participate in the divine nature and escape the corruption in the world caused by evil desires.

5 - For this very reason, make every effort to add to your faith goodness and to

goodness, knowledge, and to knowledge self-control and to self-control, perseverance, and to perseverance, godliness, and to godliness, brotherly kindness, and to brotherly kindness, love. For if you possess these qualities in increasing measure, they will keep you from being ineffective and productive, in your knowledge of our lord Jesus Christ. But if anyone does not have them, he is near-sighted and blind, and has forgotten that he has been cleansed from his past sins.

10 - Therefore my brothers be all the more eager to make your calling and election sure. For if you do these things you will never fall, and you will receive a rich welcome into the eternal kingdom, of our Lord and savior Jesus Christ.

Jah Roams in Zion

Jah roams in Zion. His love radiates out over all the trees, all the land, plants, animals and all the souls who dwell there...

Zion has no concerns of money, or Hunger or hatred.

All people living on earth, of every Nation have equal opportunity to enter Zion. This chapter is your guide to enter Zion.

Jah cleanses us

I avoided Accepting Jah into my heart for many years because I wanted to still follow an unrighteous, and sinful, and unclean lifestyle but yet , still call myself a Rasta. Every time I would start to follow Jah, he would stop me from doing many of the things in my comfortable yet sinful lifestyle. I would get the feeling my life as I knew it was *falling apart.* Looking back I now know Jah wanted to "cleanse me", so that I could become, clean and pure to enter Zion.

You may also find that once you commit yourself to *holy living*, things start to "happen". What I am really saying is...you may face many trial and tribulations. Satan may tempt you numerous times on many occasions. Just know you are not alone. This is Jah way of making us a new so that we may be purged of our old habits, and become clean as the day we were born.

#1 Depend on Jah

Jah told me plain as day one time..."Depend on me." I understood in that moment exactly what he meant. He was telling me there was no need to worry, that all I had to do was *depend on him* for all that I needed. This was very comforting, because I am the type of person who *worries about just about everything.* It is comforting to know Jah loves me enough to tell me to cast all my fears and doubts and troubles on him, and that he will work it all out for me. He wants the same thing for you too, you are his creation, his child, and Jah loves you. You cannot depend on Satan for your earthly needs and expect to enter Zion. It doesn't work like that.

How to Depend Jah

Whenever you have a problem, whenever you are unsure about something, whenever you need some guidance, or just someone to talk to...depend on Jah! Jah is always there he sees and he knows all that we feel, all that we fear, all that need and all that we desire. Depend on him.

Your 24hr direct line to Jah

You can call upon Jah any time by way of prayer. Prayer is your *24hr direct line,* straight to Jah the Almighty. If you are feeling uncertain, if you desire to have a certain type of person come into your life, if you need help with a project, pray about it, and allow Jah to provide the answer in his time, in his way. We are all Jah children his most prized creation, he wants us to pray to him... any time we have a problem. Concern, he wants us to depend on him.

#2 choose your words

What Defiles a Man
(Matthew 15:10-20)
"...**14**And when he had called all the people *unto him*, he said unto them, Hearken unto me every one *of you*, and

understand: **15**There is nothing from without a man, that entering into him can defile him: but the things which come out of him, those are they that defile the man. **16**If any man have ears to hear, let him hear..."

Do you know the words you speak, have great power? To get into Zion, we must choose our words wisely. In Zion there is no foul language, no put downs of others, no negative talk whatsoever. Zion is a place of cleanliness purity and holiness.

In the Christian bible Jah said, 'let there be light' and there was light. The bible also says that we were 'made in his image' therefore our words too, have power. Jah welcomes those into Zion who use kind words when communicating with others.

Jah shines his light favourably on those who use clean uplifting and positive words, because the earthly life is our *training and test* for our spiritual life in Zion! Watch your words...they have power to manifest.

#3 the Holy Christian Bible

As a born Rasta I can tell you much of the truth of life, and How to Enter Zion is written in the Christian bible. We as Rasta know the King James Version Christian bible is the one of the strongest "tools" available to guide and assist us to Enter Holy Mount Zion.

I recommend reading the King James Version bible from start to finish at least once, and if you read it daily that is even better. The King James version bible works when you work it! You may find that when you start to read the bible on a daily basis, Satan may try to pull you away from the path of righteousness, because he is Jealous that you have Chosen Jah - Rival and Adversary.

I read the King James Version 2 times daily. In the morning 10-15 minutes. In the even 30 mins to 1 hours. I feel spiritually clean after my bible readings. I am also more aware...that ..."*many are called...but only few shall be chosen...*"

Read your King James Version bible, and adhere to the principles...Zions Gates will be open...

#4 How to Handle Enemies

Let's face it, we all have or we have all had someone we would rather not know, or who we dislike etc. Jah wants us to strive to be the peaceful loving beings that he created us to be.

Jah knows our "Enemies" can cause us to sin...Knowing how to handle our Enemies is <u>extremely</u> important to ensure our personal entry in Zion. Our Enemies will tempt us to do things that may cause us to have a "blemish" on our Record, in Jah "book of life" ...

"...Recompense to no man evil for evil provide things honest in the sight of all men. Dearly beloved avenge not your selves, but rather give place unto wrath: For it is written, vengeance is mine, I will repay...' - **Romans 12;17** '

This bible verse is explaining that when we are obedient and keep the words, promises, and covenant of Jah, with your enemies you need not be concerned, Jah will avenge.

The next time you have an enemy and feel like you want to scream at them or perhaps do something even more than scream...just keep praying to Jah...he takes care of all things for those with a clean heart.

What else Can we do to Enter Zion?

These four tips are not the only things you can do to ensure you enter Zion, Rastafari is a way of life of which the sole purpose is live a life fitting to Enter Zion. The two More things you can do to Enter Zion are...

4 Reasons Why Rasta "Fast"

1. Acknowledge Hunger in the world

As Rastafari we fast in order to acknowledge world hunger. We do this by abstaining from eating solid food for the 24 hours during our holy Sabbath. If we eat every day, without thought for others around the world who do not have food to eat, then we on some level practice "gluttony," One of the *"7 Deadly Sins."*

2. to Recieve Favour in Jah

When we acknowledge starving and hungry men women and children around the world, by going hungry ourselves for a time, Jah looks favourably on us, as we are making a difficult "self" sacrifice, this helps to get us into Zion.

3. Teach the mind and body "Self-Control"

It is important as Rastafari to have control over our bodily *desires and urges,* so that, this way we are not an easy target for Satan's, many temptations.

Hunger can be overcome by the "power of the mind," and the living power of Jah that dwells within.

Once a week, during the holy Sabbath we as Rasta use our mind to tell the body "no" to hunger, in order that we may have mind control over the desires of our bodies. This helps us to be prepared when Satan tries to tempt us with physical desires, such as, "lust" "overeating," and "fornication."

4. Exercise the Spirit

Last but not least, another reason why Rasta "fast" during the holy Sabbath is *to practice being our spirit.*

Our spirit is active while we live our earthly lives. When we fast, our bodies become more 'light weight' as we are not digesting and processing food. Fasting in combination with other spiritual practices, allows our "spirit entity" to become stronger as while we are still earthly being, and makes us more ready to enter the spirit realm of Holy Mount Zion. Rastafari, Give Thanks.

More about the fast

Minimum 24 Fast

During this time you are not to eat any solid food. Only juices and teas may you drink. Your Rastafari Fast must be a minimum 24hrs.

Empress Yuajah

Bible Reading and Fasting

Reading the King James Version Bible on a regular basis puts Jahs law at the forefront of our minds. Reading the bible in combination with a fast creates an atmosphere of "spiritual heights." Read your bible first thing in the Morning for one hour while doing a fast, right when you wake up.

I find that because one is not processing foods, we are able to internalize the words of The Most High more readily in this manner.

You may drink some tea, while you do this or some Orange juice. I like to make myself a Huge Cup of Earl Grey tea, Every Saturday Morning...I look forward to it every Sabbath.

Meditation and Fasting

Meditating during a fast is very powerful. When you fast and you are light weight, the meditation has the ability to transcend your mind, into another state of being, or to open you up to receive guidance from The Most High Jah.

To meditate while fasting is very simple fast...and read your bible or fast and Sit in silence for at least one hour alone.

Prayer and Fasting

Prayer combined with fasting is a great way to acknowledge the creator. By praying, you tell Jah that this time is for him and by fasting he knows you have provided a sacrifice – of hunger ...of self.

I love to pray and fast during my Sabbath...It just feels good.

Fasting Alone in Silence

Jah is in the silences. Jah and his Zionly Angles are more likely to *share a message* with us when we are alone and in a quiet space, rather than when we are surrounded by others or being distracted by sounds and visual stimulation such as Television, cell phone or Radio/Stereo.

Always remember Jah lives in the Silences. Oh Jah, I and I love you. Ras-Tafari.

Invite Jah into your life

Fasting in prolonged Silence is a powerful way to invite Jah into your life. Doing these things in combination creates an environment where Jah the Creator knows he is welcome, and where you can practice being your spirit, and exercise your spiritual muscles. Practice these things on a regular basis, preferably on the Rastafari Sabbath, and you will swing the pendulum in your favour to enter Holy Mount Zion, and become a more spiritually attuned, and aware individual. *Ras-Tafari*

To learn more about the Rastafari Sabbath please read *"How to Become a Rasta" available on amazon.com*

The Meaning of Life

Only Jah can fill your heart!
Jah designed you therefore; you are
actually a spiritual being have a physical
human experience. You are a creation of
Jah. Jah dwells in you, and he loves you.

*You have a place in your heart that is only
for Jah, if you try to fill it with other things,
Alcohol, money, sex...you will forever be
empty...when you embrace Jah you will feel
full and even over-flowing...in peace,
happiness, and abundance. Jah-Rastafari*

Jah gave you Free will to choose

Had it not been for the loving power of the Almighty Jah, You would not exist today. Not only did he gave you life....he also gave you *free will*. So that you could chose to follow and keep his laws, or follow and keep the laws of another Master.

If you choose Satan, you will be tricked! Your soul will not rest in peace. If you choose Jah you walk in the light of truth, Jah will be there, from now and for eternity, Loving you, and shielding every step you take.

Jah wants you to choose him from the heart

Jah does not force you to choose him. He gently reminds you now and then, through other people, music, signs, etc. but mostly he allows the decision to live as one with him, to come from you – your own heart.

The meaning of life is to choose Jah, from your heart.

This is just a test....!

I have a secret to reveal to you my Sistrens and Idrens....This life that we are living today... of fast cars, big houses, desperate housewives...is really just a test... and so many people are failing it.

Satan loves to tempt me... I have to make sure I say "no" every time. Jah wants *clean and righteous* people in Zion. Not those who give into lustful, envious, jealous, sinful desires.

When Satan Comes around I just say "no" or <u>avoid</u> whatever it is he is in...be it a person, a drink, a movie, an encounter...the Rastafari response is always "no."

By resisting temptation Rasta <u>pass the test</u> in Babylon, and are welcome by Jah to Enter Holy Mount Zion.

Jah won't let you down!

Many People Choose Satan in life because they feel they have to. They think that if they put all their faith and all their trust in Jah...they will be disappointed...that they will not be prosperous. This is a myth....I know this because I used to believe these things myself. Satan creates illusions...in this life if we choose Jah, we will begin to see just how faithful and real he truly is. *The meaning of life...is to TRUST Jah...and allow him to reveal his love and power to you.*

a. Jah Is Prosperity and Abundance

Jah is the creator of all things. He made Heaven and earth, and Adam and Eve, and created many nations, imagine what he can do for you once you commit yourself to be his servant. Jah Job opportunities and cash flow are unlimited!

Jah is the real and biggest employer of the earth, if you choose him in this life, your own prosperity may grow beyond your wildest imagination.

Depend on Jah!

Jah wants you to depend wholly and solely on him...he will be there...he will not let you down. I have been living my life in this way for the past 2 years...and Jah Jah, is <u>my best friend,</u> and my guiding light, and he has come through for me every time *I thought he would not.* But the truth is mostly I avoid doing the things Jah doesn't like because I don't want to disappoint him, then the *bonus* is that he does come through for me....I am so blessed.

In this life if you depend on Jah, he will be there for you when you least expect it.

The true meaning of life is to live clean so that we may enter the Kingdom of <u>Zion.</u>

Thank you for reading this book on Rastafari. May Jah guide you and bless you in all good things you pursue in your life.
Blessed Love & Unity
Rastafari

Convert to Rastafari

Life as a Rasta Woman

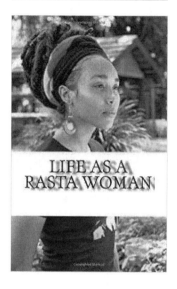

Rastafari   Prayers

Rasta Way of Life

How to Become a Rasta

Blessed Love.

Blogs

www.jamaicanlove.org
www.jamaicanloveblog.wordpress.com
www.jamaicanrastafarianlove.com

Printed in Poland
by Amazon Fulfillment
Poland Sp. z o.o., Wrocław

36992662R00139